Table of Contents

KU-246-997

Proven
Selling Skills

For Winners

Ronan McNamara

MANAGEMENT
BRIEFS

Essential Insights for Busy Managers

© 2010 Ronan McNamara
First published in 2010
ISBN 978-1-906946-02-9

Production credits
All design, artwork and liaison with printers has been undertaken by Neworld Associates,
9 Greenmount Avenue, Harold's Cross, Dublin 12, www.neworld.com

Publisher: Management Briefs, 30 The Palms, Clonskeagh, Dublin 14.

Acknowledgements

Thank you to all the people who helped me during the journey of publishing my first book.

I am grateful to Siobhan McAleer and Frank Scott-Lennon for recommending and inviting me to contribute to the Management Briefs portfolio. Thank you also to Frank Scott-Lennon and Niav McNamara for editorially guiding me with a subtle blend of expert direction, suggestion and encouragement when needed.

To the early reviewers of my initial output, Donal Cullen, Fergal Brehony and especially Eamonn Toner and Phyl Herbert, thank you for your wonderful feedback, support and ideas.

Thank you to John McInerney a 'kindred sales spirit', whose inputs, advice and direction have been so useful and appreciated.

In the last twenty years, during the course of my professional work, I have been privileged to witness the sales strategies, skills, methods, tactics and attitude of some 'top sales producers'. I salute you all and thank you for the education and for shaping my own sales thinking and doing.

To all of the sales people and managers that I have trained, who have validated the sales ideas, frameworks and tools in this book, thank you for your precious feedback.

Special thanks also to Siobhan Mc Aleer, Niamh Kelly, Fergus Gloster, Mike Kehoe and Fergal Brehony for their kind endorsements.

Finally, and especially, to my wife, Niav and children, Seán, Liam and Vlada, thank you for your ongoing support and inspiration.

Ronan McNamara

November 2010

Foreword

Ronan has written a unique book on selling skills and the reader will find within this book models, frameworks, tools, templates, ideas, approaches and tips that can be implemented to drive sales. This book is a great investment for any person who has responsibility for sales revenue.

It is a very welcome addition to our developing series of Human Resource, Organisation Behaviour and General Management Books.

All of the books in the series aim to capture the essentials for busy managers; essential knowledge and skills presented in an accessible and easy-to-read style.

A list of books already published within the series appears on the inside of the back cover. Also, on one of the last pages of the book, you will find a list of forthcoming titles which can also be viewed at our website www.ManagementBriefs.com.

We welcome any contact from you the reader; it will only improve our products and our connection to our reader population.

Frank Scott-Lennon
Series Editor
Frank@ManagementBriefs.com

November 2010

Dedication

This book is dedicated to
my late father and best 'Pal',
Michael McNamara, whose
wisdom I trust everyday.

Introduction

Introduction

"Everybody lives by selling something."

Robert Louis Stevenson 1850 -94

This book is written for salespeople who have the hunger to be successful.

The foundations of the book are laid on a great deal of practical selling and learning experience. It is written from the perspective of what salespeople need to actually do in order to be successful in selling. It is not about devising a sales strategy; it is about the face-to-face execution of the chosen selling strategy.

This book concentrates on developing winning sales behaviours.

The book starts with a chapter on the life-blood of every business - new business. The next six chapters focus entirely on the face-to-face personal selling skills of:

→ Listening

→ Questioning

→ Qualifying

→ Influencing

→ Objection handling

→ Closing

These core selling skills are then supplemented with chapters on:

→ Four specific winning sales habits

→ Leading the sales team

→ The author's selling rules

All of the tools, frameworks and advice in this book have been tried, tested and fortified in the toughest laboratory of all, the sales field. In the right hands and used the right way, your sales performance will improve.

This book is for anyone who has an interest in sales performance. The novice can learn the foundation skills and high performance tips necessary for top sales production. The experienced sales professional can refine and refresh their knowledge and sales skills. The Sales Manager or Business Owner can confidently use the guidelines, processess and tools for recruiting and leading the Sales Team.

So, if you want to improve sales performance, there is something in this book for you.

Whatever you do in sales, sell to win!

Winning New Business

1

Chapter outline
Winning New Business

→ The Challenge
→ What the Successful Sales
  Professionals Know
→ Earning the Most Commission
→ The Process of Winning New Business
→ Managing Your Own Sales Pipeline
→ Stages in a Typical Sales Pipeline
→ Knowing Your Sales Numbers
→ Cold Call Reluctance
→ How to get Appointments —
  Tips and Scripts

The Challenge

It is challenging to consistently win new business as it takes a particular skill set and mentality as well as personal traits to be successful. The ability to develop new business over the long term is really the acid test for the all-round sales professional.

The precise sales role that you fill and how you see new business is very important.

You may be:

→ A new recruit in a large organisation employed to specifically look after some of its existing customers

→ Responsible for getting new customers for the organisation

→ Responsible for a mixture of the above two sales briefs as well as developing new opportunities in a range of existing customers

The roles, responsibilities and tasks of salespeople can vary widely. Almost as varied as some of the titles you will see on their business cards e.g.

→ Account Executive

→ Sales Representative

→ Channel Sales Manager

→ Sector Sales Executive

→ National Account Manager

→ Services Sales Executive

→ Product Sales Manager

→ Territory Account Executive

Despite the range of titles, the main responsibility of these salespeople is still selling. One thing is crystal clear — the skills, attitude and processes for developing new business, remain constant. New business selling is different from selling to existing customers.

You must engage many prospects to get few signed orders. Employing the skill of qualifying will give you all-important 'cut through' so that you can make the most of your limited time. Using the telephone to qualify these prospects is also very cost effective.

> You must engage with a lot of new prospects before you get the reward of new business. It's a numbers game. Make it a quality numbers game.

Panel 1.1

What the Successful Sales Professionals Know:

Winning new business is not easy

A lot of people will say 'no' and some may even be rude

Never to take the responses personally

Winning new business is the life blood of most organisations

With enough calls, they will eventually build up a quality pipeline

To regularly check and build sales scripts

To anticipate objections and build 'pin sharp' scripts to handle them

How to modify and adapt the approach where and when necessary

Unfortunately, doing cold calls to develop new business is like studying for an exam subject that you really do not like. It takes more effort and hard work. Getting new appointments is the same. Most salespeople really dislike this part of their job so they naturally avoid the task, forgetting that this inaction has consequences for their pockets and careers.

Your attitude to cold calling will ultimately determine your success. If you:

→ Recognise that:

- by executing the process of cold calling in line with best practice, you will increase your chances of success;

- by doing it better than your competitors, you can win

→ Learn not to take the outcomes personally

→ Take full responsibility for this activity

Then you will hold the keys to your sales effectiveness.

Earning the Most Commission

In Deiric McCann's, Business Bathroom Bible, 2003, he refers to salespeople as being guilty of giving up too early; his research on this particular subject is remarkable and a summary of the findings are listed below:

Key Point

Deiric McCann asks salespeople to consider if they are guilty of giving up too early? He quotes the following statistics:

- 48% of salespeople make one call and stop

- 25% make two calls and quit on the prospect

- 15% make three calls and stop

- 12% of all salespeople go back and back and back and back

Guess which one of the above categories makes 90% of the total available commission.

The 12% group are successful salespeople who systematically seek out and select qualified leads that they will target in the marketplace. It's a campaign, not a once-off speculative call. Let's be clear here, we are not talking about high pressure salespeople manipulating buyers. We are talking about skillful salespeople who are capable of taking a straight "No" from a qualified prospect and still leaving the door ajar for a call at a future date. These professionals consistently maintain a list of high potential qualified prospects in their pipeline and commit to the process of going back and back and back to their targets. When they get their chance, they grab it and over-deliver on their commitments, thereby establishing their commercial relationship with their prospect.

Key Point

When you get a "No", the key is to be able to leave the door ajar and to follow up in the future.

The Process of Winning New Business

When the sales process breaks down, particularly in more challenging and competitive marketplaces, sales revenues drop. Having no sales process is like a professional sports person turning up for a crucial game aerobically unfit, physically injured and having 'partied' the night before. The sports person just might get away with it once, but sporting disaster looms. The sales team and salesperson who are without a clear understanding of how to execute this process are similarly in danger of failing.

Field sales is a task-intensive job. Tasks that may need to be done in a normal work day include:

→ Getting ready for an internal meeting

→ Calling out to customer X instead of customer Y

→ Dealing with e-mails

→ Reviewing new products

→ Meeting an opportunity influencer for coffee

→ Engaging a new channel partner

→ Sorting out deliveries

→ Catching up on calls/voice mails

→ Talking to marketing about a new campaign

→ Talking to accounts about that credit note

→ Changing that appointment

→ Sorting out paperwork

→ Reacting to whatever happens today

→ Meeting that tough customer for lunch

→ Attending an industry event

→ Making new cold calls

If new business is part of their remit then salespeople must be ruthless in the execution of the new business process.

Often the challenge is deciding what you are not doing today. Most field-based salespeople have a significant number of items and choices on their to-do-list and must handle them accordingly. If new business is part of their remit then they must be ruthless in the execution of the new business process. That means understanding the importance of choosing and executing the activities in the sales process.

The challenges include:

→ In order to arrange appointments you have to contact many people

→ Closing one opportunity means holding a number of meetings

→ Delivering on the numbers, activities and ratios, and rigorously qualifying every opportunity at each stage of the process, takes up a huge amount of time and effort

Key Point

Winning new business is about executing the sales process.

Managing Your Own Sales Pipeline

The sales process clearly has a number of stages and knowing where you are at each stage is crucially important. A sales pipeline for a company in a business-to-business product marketplace may have eleven distinctly different stages, e.g.

1. Suspects
2. Prospects
3. Leads
4. Contacted
5. Appointment
6. Gathering Information
7. Formal Quote
8. Verbal Decision
9. Signed Orders
10. Product/Service delivery
11. Paid – Customer's cheque clearing in the bank account.

Stages in a Typical Sales Pipeline

Stage	Definition
Suspects	The sum total of the opportunities in your marketplace.
Prospects	The target market that you intend to pursue – usually by means of a combination of promotional marketing activities that may culminate in a targeted and personalised mailshot. At this stage the salesperson has not contacted the person or organisation.
Leads	The prospects that you intend to contact, usually by phone and/or people who have responded directly to promotional marketing activity.
Contacted	This is the stage in the pipeline where there are people who you have contacted but do not yet have a firm appointment with. These will include the firm 'nos' who may after time be re-classified as prospects. Look at them as "I have contacted them, they said a firm 'No', but I will contact them again in the future."
Appointment	At this stage appointments have been scheduled.
Gathering information	This stage is included for sales organisations who typically will not get all the information they need to be able to make a formal quote. A lot of commodity sales organisations will be able to bypass this stage to the next one.
Formal Quote	At this stage, the prospect has physically received a quote.
Verbal Decision	This stage indicates that the salesperson has been given a verbal yes, but is waiting for paperwork or further confirmation.
Signed Orders	A contract has now been signed but may still be subject to internal organisational approval. From an organisational perspective you need to execute the next two stages as well.
Delivery	The product/service has been delivered to the prospect.
Getting Paid	The prospect's cheque has cleared in the bank and they have just officially become a customer. The last act in going from prospect to customer!

The pipeline stages can be further modified for work-flow and organisational effectiveness whereby data collected during the sales process may be used to update the billing system as the opportunity moves from suspect stage through to becoming a customer.

It is important to focus on moving the opportunities on to the next stage, backwards or out of the pipeline altogether. This discipline will make your sales pipeline predictable and strong.

Look at how dates are naturally linked in a sales pipeline – a date for: a direct mailshot, a phone call, actual contact, an agreed appointment, collecting all the information needed to quote, expecting a verbal decision, getting a signed order. There is a natural flow to a pipeline and so it is with dates and events in the process of winning a sale.

Key Point

Each pipeline stage in the sales process should be marked by an event and date.

Understanding the process is just one aspect to managing pipelines. Knowing your numbers is critical for hitting your sales target. These numbers are ratios, commonly referred to as a 'close rate'. This rate is built up over time and actually established by the daily habits of the salesperson.

Gary Player, the world-renowned South African Golfer, famously said *"The more I practise, the luckier I get."*

Imagine the salesperson who thinks:

> **"The more doors I knock on, the luckier I get"**

An accurate understanding of each of the stages in the sales pipeline will clearly highlight the activities that you need to concentrate on. This is one of the best tools for managing sales success. It can be applied at individual, team and organisational level.

Knowing Your Sales Numbers

The following questions must be answered in order to verify a salesperson's *'close rate'* when cold-calling:

→ How many phone-calls do you have to make to get one appointment?

→ How many appointments do you have to make to get a sale?

In establishing these ratios, it is advisable to start by looking at just one average new business sale. Take for example new business salespeople who, to get one sale, need four appointments and, on average, have to make ten telephone calls to get one appointment.

These salespeople have a 'close rate' of 40:4:1 as shown in the table below:

Number of telephone calls	40
Number of appointments	4
Number of resulting sales	1

If this salesperson has a monthly target of eight deals per month, then they will have basic activity targets that will clearly show them what 'on average' they need to do if they maintain their current habits (four week month assumed).

These ratios will vary from industry to industry and salesperson to salesperson. The main variable within industries is the skill levels of the salespeople in qualifying their opportunities. Some will always be more realistic than others. Consequently they will choose to invest most of their time on the opportunities that give them the strongest chance of winning. The salesperson and manager can get a very clear picture of the requirements for hitting the sales target e.g. The salesperson must have 32 appointments per month generated, by making an average of 320 phone calls per month.

Key Point

Know your sales call ratios.

Cold Call Reluctance

Mentioning cold call reluctance to a group of salespeople is like talking about the 'elephant in the room.' The most consistent cause of lack of sales success is, lack of activity. Some of the common causes of this are:

Situation	Salesperson feels
Lack of product or business knowledge	Not knowing makes me feel stupid
Over preparation	I need more information before I call
Hearing the word 'No' too often	I do not like consistent rejection
Exposure and risk	I feel uncertain because I do not know them
Arrogance	I don't do cold calls – that's for little people
New ground	I've never done this before
Not a people person	I don't really like people, why should I talk to new ones
Procrastination	I will do it tomorrow
Full Pipeline	I'm on target, I can stop cold calling

The main reasons for salespeople failing to take responsibility for developing new business are fear of failure, rejection and embarrassment.

This can be overcome by developing or changing their:

→ Knowledge of their product/ service, organisation and marketplace

→ Knowledge of how important the task is

→ Attitude towards prospecting

Also, by giving them the tools, motivation and environment to do the job.

How to get Appointments – Tips and Scripts

The first step is to identify prospects and then to make contact by phone in order to set up meetings. You must now make a direct approach, carefully and effectively, in order to get face-to-face with as many of them as possible.

You must first introduce yourself to prospects giving them your name, company and reason for your call. Following this introductory statement, you have to hold their attention by explaining how you may be able to help them if you arrange a meeting.

Then ask for an appointment. This can be achieved by showing how you may be able to help them.

Remember, the only objective is to get into their diary, so do not try to sell over the phone. Some examples:

Panel 1.2

Approach on a Cold Call

"Good morning. May I speak to David Clarke"
(Do not use Mr, Miss, etc..)

"David, are you free to speak for a moment?"

"Yes"

"David, my name is ...., I work with X company.

"We provide a range of services specifically designed for businesses like yours to increase your sales. Would you invest just ten minutes to see if we can do this for you? If, after ten minutes, we do not have middle ground, we can stop the meeting.

David, would Tuesday at 10am or Thursday at 2pm suit you best? Just ten minutes to see if your sales can be improved?"

Another option for, say a territory salesperson, is to tell prospects that you are in the area on a specific day and that you regularly visit that area so if you don't get the appointment they can expect another call to seek another appointment. This approach is for territory representatives only and needs to be skillfully communicated.

Of course, the prospects will have objections and it is up to us to handle these as they arise.

Some tips on handling appointment-making objections

There are only a few basic objections that a prospect can raise so why not learn them in advance and how to overcome

them. Again preparation is the key.

Note that in the following examples each one is always followed by the alternative close: the question is *"When can I see you?"* not *"Will you see me?"* Always ask for the appointment.

"What's it about?"

That is why I am telephoning you David, so that we can arrange to get together because I can show you much better than I can tell you. So, would Monday at ... or Tuesday at .. suit you best?

"Send me details?"

Certainly, I could send you details Paul, but they need to be tailor-made to suit your company's particular

14

requirements. That is why I would like to meet you in person first.

So, would Monday at... or Tuesday at... suit you best?

"I'm too busy"

Paul, I appreciate you are a busy man, which is why I telephoned to make an appointment rather than just call on you personally. So, would Monday at... or Tuesday at ... suit you best?

"I'm not interested"

David, I can appreciate you not being interested in something you have not yet seen. However, so that you can make a fair assessment of what we offer, I would like to share just ten minutes with you. So, would Monday at... or Tuesday at... suit you best?

"Are you selling something?"

David, we provide a service. The first priority is to establish whether our services will be of benefit to you. You will be able to judge that for yourself very quickly. If we do not have common ground after ten minutes we can stop the meeting and save both of us time. So, would Thursday at 2pm or Friday at 3pm suit you best?

"What will it cost?"

It costs nothing to talk with me David. Our first priority is to see if I can be of benefit to you. So, would Monday at... or Tuesday at... suit you best?

The Road Ahead

Once you get that all important first meeting with the prospect you can then start the process of selling to the prospect using your all important personal selling skills.

The remainder of this book is dedicated to those personal selling skills, four winning sales habits and leading the sales team. The book concludes with a collection of selling rules that will guide your success.

Summary of Chapter 1

→ New business is a numbers' game

→ The best sales people know 'new business sales' are not easy

→ Manage your own sales pipeline

→ Know your sales call ratios

→ Beware of cold call reluctance

→ Build, develop and use scripts to get appointments

2 Listening Skills

Chapter outline
Listening Skills

→ Listening Skills for the
   Professional Salesperson
→ Passive Listening
→ Passive Listening Triggers
→ Interactive Listening
→ Active Listening for Winning Sales
→ An Active Listening Tool

Listening Skills for the Professional Salesperson

One of the most important skills a professional salesperson can have is the ability to listen. It is a very underrated skill, and yet, if developed, it can be the main reason behind a salesperson's success.

Most salespeople, because they are in sales, believe that their own listening skills are good, if not excellent. It is the listening habits that salespeople develop over time that are important. Most humans tend to listen less as time passes and they become more experienced and confident in the subject matter. Remember how carefully you drove a car when you first learned to drive and think how many bad habits have probably crept in by now.

Key Point

When your listening wanes you will miss the message.

Many salespeople have the conviction that selling is primarily about product knowledge, knowledge of your organisation and how well you handle customers' questions. Wrong! Whilst these are important parts of your selling tool box, they are not the most important.

Key Point

The ability to understand exactly where your customers are coming from, where they intend to go and how they feel, will give you a solid foundation to sell effectively.

Excellent listening skills will help you to develop empathy — the ability to understand your prospect's position and how it makes him/her feel.

Case Study

In the 1980s, David Hairman was a legendary salesman in Wang Computers. He was consistently the most successful and a true champion salesperson.

Upon meeting this 'sales legend', I asked him for his top three tips for success in sales. Imagine my surprise when, pointing to both his ears he replied "Two of these and (pointing to his mouth) one of those." He did this three times.

Being a novice salesman at the time, I quizzed him further — "What do you mean?" He answered:

"How can you possibly sell something to anybody if you do not know exactly what it is they are looking for?"

My view of selling was forever turned on its head. Here was a proven sales expert advocating talking as little as possible. This has helped me to be able to clearly understand the difference between 'Tell Sell' sales amateurs and 'Client-centred' sales professionals.

The former dominate the opening exchanges with their prospects with facts about themselves, their product and their organisation. They are utterly self-focused. The latter, concentrate on their prospects' situations, wants and needs, focusing on where their prospects currently are and where they wish to get to. The difference between them is the mark of a true sales professional.

There are three main types of listening:

1. Passive

2. Interactive

3. Active

Passive Listening

Passive listening is a state that most people are fully familiar with even if they are not aware of it. Passive listening occurs when you are physically present in front of someone who is talking, but your mind wanders off to a different place — that place could be the weekend you are about to go on or it could be thoughts about the next meeting that you have, or even a social event that you have planned.

This is an unsettling place for salespeople to find themselves in.

Consider the circumstances — you are with a customer and you are thinking about something else. This happens because of the way the human brain is built. Our brain is physically capable of processing six hundred words per minute — that is literally the 'speed of thought.' Our amazing central processing unit — brain capability — thinks at three times the rate of a fast speaker who communicates at a typical rate of two hundred words per minute. That leaves a lot of processing capacity free to look for other matters to process. You could be daydreaming. In a lot of instances, the subject occupying your thoughts may be a lot more absorbing than what your customer or prospect may be saying or you may be trying to 'second guess' what your customer is going to say next. Either way, you are not in the 'here and now.'

If you are in this zone, you are in danger of a bad moment of truth. The customer could quickly form an opinion that you are not really listening and that maybe you don't care. This is equivalent to inviting the customer to seek an alternative vendor/salesperson — who will pay more attention to him/her.

This situation of wandering attention can occur when you are physically tired or under pressure or if you are dealing with a lot of customers where conversations can become very predictable. Consider, for a moment, a situation when you return home after a long day at work to meet your partner/spouse – typically, you can predict the conversation to an accurate degree, your brain wanders, seeking more challenging information, your eyes glaze over and you miss an important point that has just been made. You are then accused of not listening and have to suffer the consequences – perhaps in silence! It goes without saying that you do not want to end up in a similar position with your prospects/customers.

It is very important to understand what passive listening is, watch out for it and correct it whilst with your prospects and customers.

Key Point

Passive listening will cost you sales, earnings and money; and perhaps even friendships.

Passive Listening Triggers

Meeting a prospect for the first time always promotes a certain level of anxiety. A typical salesperson is usually desperately trying to establish a firm middle ground as quickly as possible. Many flounder badly at this and quickly get labelled as 'not worthy of doing business with' and are processed out the door by the prospect.

The initial stage when you meet your prospect in reception and are walking to an office for the meeting, is the small-talk stage. Most salespeople will talk about one or more of the following: the weather, the traffic, journey and/ or sport.

These can be 'passive listening triggers' in so far as they may trigger the prospect into listening passively and/or probably switching off their listening altogether. The quickest way to be associated with the amateurs, *in the mind of your prospect,* is to do and say the same things as these amateurs. Prospects typically do not have a high regard for most salespeople.

Let's look at things from our prospect's perspective. It is quite likely that the prospect has a view or an opinion on salespeople based upon experience, perhaps as a disappointed consumer and/ or professional buyer. It may come as no surprise that the view of a 'typical salesperson' is far from complimentary.

The following labels have been stuck on salespeople:

→ Aggressive

→ In a rush

→ Late

→ Smarmy

→ Economical with the truth

→ A talker

→ Out to get you

→ Unprofessional

→ Pushy

→ Untrustworthy

That is not quite the company that the professional salesperson wants to be associated with. The professional salesperson goes through the same sales process as the amateurs — calling to get appointments, arranging meetings, information gathering, presenting and closing. In order to disassociate yourself from the amateurs, you must make sure that you do not do or say the same things as them. In order to stand out, differentiate yourself through your consistent professionalism.

Key Point

Aim to consistently **stand out** from the pack in all that you do!

Professional salespeople should never talk about weather, traffic and sport, unless the prospect introduces the subject. If you are looking for middle ground, ask an open question about their 'comfort zone':

→ The business's locations/ addresses

→ The business/organisation

→ The person's job/role and responsibilities

→ The person's immediate team or manager

Key Point

It often takes only ninety seconds for a person to start forming an opinion about another person and only three minutes for them to crystallise that opinion.

Do not waste this crucial time talking about the same things as the amateurs. Get the prospect talking. You may just get to hear some very useful information.

Interactive Listening

Interactive listening is a very natural listening state. With interactive listening there is a dialogue; listening and talking in equal measures by both parties. It is most suitable to an informal setting like chatting over a cup of coffee or at the start and end of meetings when small-talk is acceptable.

It is not acceptable if customers are discussing their business situation, because every time you talk, you are not listening. If they are talking about themselves, their team, their organisation, their problems and challenges, then active listening is essential to a successful meeting.

Many sales people who think they have a solution to a prospect's problem, pre-empt or anticipate what the person is going to say and jump in too quickly to talk about their solution without hearing the full story or facts from the prospect. Again, you are in danger of transmitting the wrong message to your prospects that you are not listening (or possibly even, interrupting), so they should really consider an alternative supplier who might actually listen to them.

The danger with interactive listening is that it is very natural for salespeople and they are usually very good at it (having a chat). However, it can be counter productive, talking while the prospect is trying to tell you something that could prove crucial to helping them and winning their business.

Key Point

Listen twice as much as you talk.

Active Listening for Winning Sales

Active listening is so-called because you fully engage 'both sides' of your brain in the conversation.

Experimentation has shown that the different sides, or hemispheres, of the brain are responsible for different ways of thinking. Most individuals have a distinct preference for one of these.

Left Brain	Right Brain
Logical	Feelings / emotions
Sequential	Random
Rational	Intuitive
Analytical	Imaginative
Objective	Subjective
Looks at parts	Looks at wholes/ entities

When you are actively listening to prospects you are really concentrating on what they are saying and how they are saying it — you are using both the left and right sides of your brain. This allows you to understand your prospects' logical positions as well as how it makes them feel. This is empathy.

You are also in the present tense, the 'here and now'. You are devoting your attention to what the prospects/customers are saying now. You are not 'second guessing' what they are going to say next and working out your answer at the same time. It is very much about being alive to the conversation right now.

Active listening is about really hearing what your prospects are saying and how they are saying it. Listen for any emotion so that you can understand the real meaning of the words e.g. a close customer might say "Frank is leaving my team." On paper, written down, this is very black and white. However, the way that the customer says it, will tell you

22

a lot, if you are actively listening, that is.

Be warned, active listening requires real concentration and this can be difficult to sustain over a long period of time. Listening properly and intently demands a lot of energy.

Remember it is impossible to actively listen all the time. So, in your quieter moments, like in the car, enjoy passively listening to the radio.

Key Point

When you are listening, focus on the 'here and now.'

An Active Listening Tool

Here is a useful tool for helping you to develop your active listening skills when customers or prospects are talking with you:

Reply to the content of what has been said

Accept how the situation makes them feel

Demonstrate to them you have been listening

Agree on the proposed next steps

Ask is there anything else?

Let's look at each stage in more detail.

REPLY exactly to what your prospects/customers have said. You may have news for them but listen to what they are saying first. Do not try to avoid what your prospects are saying. So, if they are not sure or happy about something, deal with that first before you deliver your news.

Then, if they make the point by expressing a feeling; e.g. 'I'm under pressure', 'I'm not happy', 'We are up against a deadline', 'We are delighted with...', 'I like...', make sure that you under-pin their feelings by **ACCEPTING**

and acknowledging their feelings explicitly.

e.g. I fully understand why that is putting you under pressure and how important it is to meet the upcoming deadline.

Next, you should clearly **DEMONSTRATE** to the prospect that you have been listening. This is a great opportunity to differentiate yourself from most of your competitors. You can show your prospects you have been listening by paraphrasing what they said.

When we paraphrase what the prospects said, we simply put it in our own words. The other option is to summarise what they have said, then discuss and **AGREE** the next steps. This should also help confirm your understanding of the situation. This gives the professional salesperson the opportunity to build a deeper rapport and understanding with their prospects.

The final element when actively listening to your customer is to simply **ASK** them:

Is there anything else that we at (your organisation's name) can help you with?

This is a very powerful little question. In the right hands and used skilfully it can send very clear signals to your customers. If the customers have other issues or opportunities, they just might discuss them with you simply because you asked. They will certainly consider discussing these topics with you at the next meeting.

Key Point

The best way to monitor your listening skills on an ongoing basis is to use the 'coffee cup test.'

When having coffee with your customer, be very conscious of how empty or full your cup

is, during the conversation. If your cup is still full after five minutes, this means you have been doing all the talking and have not made time to listen. This is a great reminder to listen twice as much as you talk.

Summary of Chapter 2

→ Passive listening has many dangers for salespeople

→ Avoid switching off your prospect with passive listening triggers

→ Use interactive listening with your prospects and customers when chatting and building relationships. Always use active listening when discussing their business

→ Use the 'Reply, Accept, Demonstrate, Agree, Ask' method and 'Coffee Cup' test for listening and monitoring

→ Listening properly gives you the information needed to sell successfully

→ Listen twice as much as you talk!

Questioning Skills

3

Chapter outline
Questioning Skills

→ The Art of Questioning
→ The Funnelling Questioning Technique
→ A Questioning Framework
→ Getting the Information You Need to Sell Effectively
→ The Power of 'How?' and 'What?'
→ An Agenda for Success

The Art of Questioning is to:

"Seek first to understand, then to be understood."

So said Stephen Covey in his ground-breaking book about personal leadership and management called 'The Seven Habits of Highly Effective People' (1989). Habit number five, *"Seek first to understand and then to be understood"* promotes the principle of mutual understanding but focuses us first on understanding the other person. It is a principle and tool that serves the professional salesperson extremely well.

The Funnelling Questioning Technique

Funnelling questioning refers to using specific types of questions to guide a conversation from general to specific. The focus of the conversation goes from broad to narrow and is represented by the diagram below.

Panel 3.1

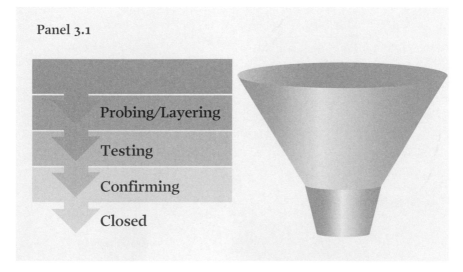

Probing/Layering

Testing

Confirming

Closed

There are a range of different types of questions that can be used in the communication process. The continuum runs from open to closed questions but can also move from closed to open. As you would expect, these are complete opposites.

Closed questions

A closed question is a direct question to which there are only two possible responses — yes or no, there is no possible in-between response. There is clarity! A classic closed question like 'Do you have a budget?' is likely to only receive a 'yes or no' answer.

Many salespeople start their initial dialogues with direct closed questions, leaving the prospects feeling under attack. This may result in prospects not wanting to talk to you – not very helpful if you are trying to sell them something. This occurs because salespeople, seeking to anchor conversations, will steer the dialogues to their own comfort zones (and not their prospects'). Consequently salespeople will ask questions like some of the following:

→ Are you interested in X?

→ Do you purchase X?

→ Have you got a budget for X?

→ Will you order X this month?

Understand this crucial point – the above questions are of course important, but, because they are closed questions, they do not allow the customer to be expansive and may negatively impact on the all-important information-gathering and rapport-building process.

Key Point

Start new conversations with new prospects with open questions or open requests for information.

Panel 3.2
A Questioning Framework

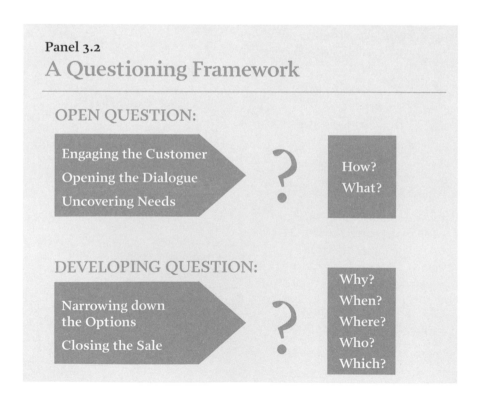

OPEN QUESTION:

Engaging the Customer

Opening the Dialogue

Uncovering Needs

? How? What?

DEVELOPING QUESTION:

Narrowing down the Options

Closing the Sale

? Why? When? Where? Who? Which?

Open questions

Rudyard Kipling called the questions: Who? What? Where? Why? When? and How?; his best friends, because they taught him all that he knew. They can all be used for asking open questions in initial conversations with prospects.

In the sales arena, the first crucial step is to gather as much information as possible. Open questions are the best means of achieving this task. You are effectively inviting a person to talk about a topic in a very non-invasive way. Examples of these types of questions are given below.

Open questions can also be used to uncover prospects' hidden objections. Hidden objections are when prospects don't reveal to prospective sellers what is the real problem in their organisation when making purchasing decisions. From a selling perspective, it will take skill and patience to break down this initial barrier. Consider how doctors operate; the best of them are extremely skilled at getting patients to do most of the talking during the early stage of a diagnosis. They are gathering as much information from the patient as possible before making their decision on the best course of action. As a tool for gathering information in a sales engagement, this perspective is very useful, particularly in more complex sales that involve many factors like multiple products, services and people. Other salespeople have described this process to me as peeling an onion layer by layer, or probing/layering.

Probing/Layering Questions

This process of uncovering the real pain or motivation of the prospect could be visualised as the prospect giving you another layer of information e.g. a prospect may say *"You are more expensive!"* A probing/layering question is *"Tell me, what do you mean by more expensive?"* The prospect may then give you an insight that will allow you to reposition your offering and allow you to close the sale.

Testing Questions

A testing question allows you to test your understanding of the current situation: *"So, what you're saying is this product needs to be delivered within two weeks?"* A testing question, asked the right way, will get the prospect to elaborate and give you more information.

Confirming Questions

A confirming question is designed to cement your understanding of the actual situation: *"Why do you want to order just 6 boxes now?"*

Getting the Information You Need to Sell Effectively

Often the professional salesperson will have clear information objectives (not to be confused with preconceived ideas) going into the meeting, such as aiming to discover:

→ How much is the prospect's budget?

→ When do they need this completed by?

→ Who really makes the decisions?

The salesperson needs to get that information, but cannot possibly start the conversation with three closed questions. Prospects automatically become more defensive and guarded when asked three or more closed questions in succession. The last thing salespeople want is for their prospects to 'dry up' regarding the information they are willing to share. So, what they need to do is to start the conversation in a very understanding way and to try and tune into a prospect's wavelength before asking closed questions. Use an open question to break the ice.

An open question invites a response to a **relevant** question that has been asked respectfully and politely. The more considered and intelligent the questions, the better. These types of questions are much more difficult to construct in a face-to-face

meeting so do your preparation in advance.

"What kind of a priority do you and your colleagues give this project?" may eventually lead to the topic of the budget.

With open questions, we are very much at the first stage of Covey's fifth habit *'Seek first to understand.'* We are seeking the following information.

→ What are the main goals for your organisation in the next year?

→ How do you plan to achieve them?

→ What do you think are the most important factors governing the success of these plans?

The last thing salespeople want is for their prospects to 'dry up' regarding the information they are willing to share.

Key Point

Tips for asking questions during the sales process:

1. Ask open questions at the start of the meeting.

2. Ask a small number of quality questions. Have targeted questions that lead to discussion.

3. Don't ask leading questions that bring the customer to the answer, eg do you think our offer is fair?

4. Leave intimate questions until rapport has been established. You need access before you ask these.

5. Ask the right questions at the right time. Postpone if the other person is not ready.

6. Only ask questions that you wouldn't be expected to know the answer to. "How many employees?" -is the ultimate question to declare to the prospect that you have not prepared properly for this meeting.

Using the above list will remind you to use best practice when getting your prospects to openly discuss their situation, so that you can qualify whether a prospect is worth further investment in terms of time and effort.

In a face-to-face situation with a new prospect, you should be trying to get specific information that is not already in the public domain. When requesting information from business people who work for large organisations that typically have a high profile, it helps to get them talking within their comfort zone; once you identify one of the comfort zones, then ask open questions.

Sample Question 1

"I am aware that there is a lot of information in the public domain about your organisation. How do you see it and what needs to happen next?"

Please understand the above is not a 'one pill cures everything' approach. It is simply an approach that gets new prospects talking and thereby gives you the ammunition to sell. The choice of language is very important and must be appropriate. You need to develop this repertoire so that it is industry and individually appropriate to the situation. In a more casual meeting you can use the above approach but with different language, such as below.

Sample Question 2

"There is a lot of news in the papers about your industry. What's going on and what does it really mean?"

The Power of 'How?' and 'What?', with a Little Bit of 'Why?'

The use of open questions that focus on 'How?' and 'What?' are the most powerful. You can continue a conversation, and thereby your information gathering, in a very constructive way. The key is to keep those conversations customer oriented. The questions should be directed at the particular individual, the individual's team and the individual's organisation. The following are good examples:

→ What are you trying to achieve?

→ How do you think you can get there?

→ What do you think is most important?

→ How focused is the whole organisation on this?

Again, we must think of the application and appropriateness of the above powerful open questions. The focus must be on prospects' issues as they perceive them.

Opening with 'How' and 'What' questions combined with some 'Why' questions are a powerful method for learning about prospects' needs wants and motivations.

Key Point

'How?' and 'What?', with a little bit of 'Why?' are powerful questions for developing conversations.

An Agenda for Success

For large opportunities with new prospects, the initial objectives are to get as much information as possible and to differentiate yourself from other salespeople who are chasing this opportunity.

In terms of preparation for the initial meeting, drawing up a formal agenda is strongly recommended. This agenda will create a good impression, putting the prospect at ease and helping you to achieve your objectives. The agenda should be printed on high quality headed paper and clearly marked 'Draft Agenda.'

Introduce the agenda along the lines of: 'I have taken the liberty of preparing a draft agenda for the meeting. Can you please have a look at it to see if I have overlooked anything?'

The Draft Agenda should be formatted as follows:

DRAFT AGENDA

NAMES OF THEIR ORGANISATION AND YOUR ORGANISATION

NAMES AND TITLES OF ALL INVOLVED IN THE MEETING

LOCATION

DATE

MEETING OBJECTIVE: e.g. For their organisation and your organisation to explore middle ground with a view to addressing X in their organisation.

INTRODUCTIONS AND BACKGROUND:

Their organisation
Your organisation

DISCUSSION/Q&A

AOB

NEXT STEPS

This is a fail-safe way to differentiate yourself from the competition and create that all-important positive first impression. Some may view this as being a little old fashioned, but in today's market place, people are starting to put more currency on old fashioned values.

Use this as a sales tool as it allows the prospect to be comfortable at the start about the scope and direction of the meeting. It also helps to get the prospect talking first and is very useful for recording important issues as they arise during the meeting for later feedback, decisions and follow up by e-mail. Finally, it will help to steer the direction that the meeting is going in.

This is an excellent way to start important meetings with prospects and is particularly useful for larger opportunities. You will get the prospect talking. Try it and remember to listen twice as much as you talk.

Summary of Chapter 3

→ In selling, first find out what is going on

→ Open questions give you the information you need to sell effectively

→ Use the Funnelling Questioning Technique

→ 'How?' and 'What?', with a little bit of 'Why?' are the most useful questions for developing conversations

→ A well structured agenda will create a positive first impression

→ Get the prospect talking first

→ Remember to listen.

Qualifying Skills

4

Chapter outline
Qualifying Skills

→ C MAGNETS — Saving You Time, Money and Effort

→ C MAGNETS: Competition? Money? Authority? Goals? Needs? Encourage Objections? Timescale? Solution and Size?

→ The Greatest Waste of a Salesperson's Time

→ Qualifying Prospects During the Sales Cycle

→ Using C MAGNETS for Sales Success

→ How and When to Use C MAGNETS

C MAGNETS — Saving You Time, Money and Effort

C MAGNETS is a magnet for attracting prospects and customers you wish to sell to.

Panel 4.1

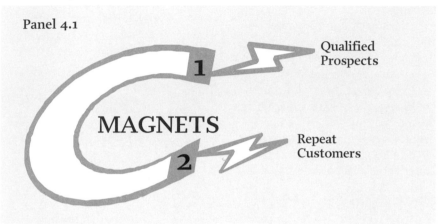

C MAGNETS stands for:

Competition?

Money?

Authority?

Goals?

Needs?

Encourage Objections?

Timescale?

Solution and Size?

At the end of every sales year, sales quarter, sales month and week the universal cry from salespeople all over the world is "If I had more time, I could have sold more." Ask salespeople "What is your greatest waste of time?", they usually answer:

→ Traffic and driving to meet clients

→ Paperwork and completing reports

→ Internal meetings and prospects who waste time

While there are technology responses to these challenges like conference calling, telesales, hand-held devices, laptops, automatic ordering systems, GPS, etc. None of these addresses the core time challenge.

The Greatest Waste of a Salesperson's Time

'Qualifying' is one of the most used words in the sales environment. Unfortunately, it is also one of the most misunderstood. Ask a fledgling salesperson or a proven sales warrior, "Is that lead qualified?" Both may say "yes", but the reality is, one thinks that he/she is about to set up a first meeting with a customer and the other may think he/she is about to get the signed order. As sales specialists, you need to be very clear exactly what constitutes a qualified sales lead.

Key Point

Before and during the sales process, ask yourself, "Is this prospect 'fit' for purpose?"

Your organisation is about to invest significant resources trying to turn the prospect into a paying customer. So, *'Is the prospect fit for the investment of time and effort?'* is the right question to ask. But how to get the correct answer is the real challenge. Understanding qualifying and applying this wonderful sales tool — C MAGNETS - will deliver the right answer to you in over 99% of applications.

Many salespeople approach the task of 'reaching their targets' by being as busy as possible. Their philosophy is to create as much activity as possible — in terms of meetings and quotations etc.

— and hope that some of it ends up successful. Sometimes this approach will deliver results, depending on market conditions and the selling company's market offering. This approach is very common in a long-run, bull market. This usually reinforces the sales behaviour and results become more volatile as markets and business confidence turn.

Key Point

If you 'close' one in five opportunities i.e. 20%, then, on average, you are wasting 80% of your time — that adds up to a lot of investment.

How many salespeople ask their prospects in the initial stages of the sales engagement:

→ Would you like a quote?

→ Would you like a proposal?

→ Would you like to meet again next month?

→ Would you like me to get you information?

→ Would you like a detailed specification?

→ Would you like to meet one of our specialist staff?

All these questions add up to "Would you like some free consulting or up to date information on specifications and prices?" Rarely do people turn down free information when it is offered to them. Prospects will do their job and say "yes."

New sales recruits are typically guilty of generating a lot of this proposal paperwork and effort, as they seek to please as many prospects as possible, and get busy in their new jobs. The proposals start to become more 'cut and paste', less personalised, less focused and more ineffective. The volume of paperwork increases as the busy salesperson responds to as many opportunities as is physically possible. Lots of solid hard work with no real focus other than 'if I keep doing this then some of it will stick.' What about solid hard work with focus?

C MAGNETS is an extremely useful tool. It allows you to establish early on with a customer whether you are likely to make the sale or not. This enables you to identify early, those prospects that will end up in an inevitable 'No' and avoid wasting considerable time and effort by qualifying out of a sales opportunity early in the sales cycle.

Qualifying Prospects During the Sales Cycle

Key Point

Every sales opportunity should be qualified at every stage of the sales process.

The elements of C MAGNETS are:

Competition?

As a salesperson, you must ask yourself one simple question:

→ Do I know the competition and can I beat them?

It is important that the salesperson gets an up-to-date view on 'how' the current supplier is viewed. Is there a genuine opportunity, or is the salesperson going through the process of giving the prospects up-to-date pricing so that they can use this information to reduce pricing from a supplier that they are actually happy with? A realistic answer and score at the earliest stage in the sales cycle will save you a lot of wasted investment over your sales career. The good news is that it will give you a lot more time to sell to those prospects where you have a better chance of success.

Money?

'Will they pay us if we supply them?'

Money is one of the most taboo subjects in the world. One reason is because most people understand what it is like to be short of money. Consequently, salespeople are conditioned long before they get into selling to avoid the subject of money. As a result, many salespeople will only talk about money late in the sales cycle. This is a particularly dangerous practice. If we leave the subject of money until late in the sales cycle, we are in danger of expending a great deal of effort before we find out that the prospect either has none, or has no intention of spending your proposed figure in the acquisition of your company's products/services.

The best practice to qualify a prospect is to bring the topic of money into the conversation at the earliest possible opportunity. A frank discussion about the prospect's possible budget and your ball park figure goes a long way towards finding out if the prospect is really serious about proceeding to the next step. Of course, subtlety and skill are required in this regard.

The following questions can produce particularly revealing answers and can be especially helpful in qualifying prospects at an early stage.

→ Have you budgeted for this project?

→ How does the budget process work in your organisation?

→ Does this spend come out of a department budget?

Key Point

When it comes to Money, there are two questions:

- Has your prospect got any?

- Will they pay you?

The answers are crucial in deciding whether to invest more time with this prospect or not.

Authority?

'Am I selling to the person who has the authority to sign this order?'

If you are not, you must make the valid assumption that your competitor is and that they are in a much stronger position than you are. In fact, you can be confident that, in the vast majority of cases, you are not going to get the deal. You may finish an honourable second but the only role you are currently filling is giving the organisation valid information so that they can negotiate harder with your competition, their existing supplier.

The next step is to make sure that you get access to the decision maker. The easiest way to do this is to call on decision makers as high up the organisation as possible. Proactively doing this is much better than being asked to quote by a non-decision-maker.

Key Point

It is easier to be introduced down an organisation than get introduced up the organisation.

On new prospects, be very selective where you first call and how you get to the decision makers. Judicious use of some of the following questions will help you find out who the key decision maker is:

→ How are purchase orders processed in your organisation?

→ Is the decision an individual or committee one?

→ Who is on the committee and

who is the influencer in the committee?

→ Does one person take responsibility for this type of purchase?

→ Who signs the Purchase Order?

Key Point

When it comes to Authority:

Make sure you are in front of the decision makers; otherwise all you are doing is providing free consulting,and wasting your valuable sales time.

Goals?

'Do I know the specific goals of:

→ the individual decision maker,

→ the team they are in, and

→ the organisation?'

This element of C MAGNETS is intended to evaluate larger, more complex opportunities. It is a broad question, but clarity with larger opportunities will guide you as to whether:

→ you should invest time and energy on the opportunity

→ your resources are currently better invested elsewhere.

The best way to find out these goals is to ASK the decision makers. That way you find out what is really going on and can decide to qualify in and focus on the opportunity. Alternatively, you can decide that the large investment is not worth the risk and qualify out. It is important to receive an answer on all three levels of the question — this will help you to establish early in the sales cycle if the prospect has a compelling reason to act.

Needs?

'Do I understand the needs of the prospect better than the competition does?'

To understand prospects properly, you must be able to:

→ Articulate precisely the nature of their needs from *their* perspective

→ Prioritise their needs from *their* perspective

→ Weight their needs from *their* perspective

To do this requires an in-depth discussion and analysis with a prospect. If you can complete the above three stages through a consultative selling approach with your prospect, then the deal is yours to win.

'Do I understand the needs of the prospect better than the competition does?'

41

Key Point

When it comes to **Needs**:

- Ask yourself are you able to articulate your prospects' needs, priortise them and weight them from their perspective?
- If you can, then the deal is yours to win (or lose).

Clearly the prospects are your best source of information.

- Make sure you are in front of them gathering information, presenting and closing.

Encourage Objections?

This question is three-fold:

→ Have the prospects raised objections?

→ Have I dealt with these objections?

→ If not, have I encouraged objections from them?

If, during the course of the sales conversations, the prospect has not raised any objections, then it is up to you to find them. Just because prospects have not articulated any objections to you, it does not mean that they do not have any. These type of objections are called hidden objections and they are like snakes, lying quietly in the grass, waiting to sneak up on you. Hidden objections must be dealt with if you are to be successful in closing the sales opportunity. Chapter six will outline the importance of dealing with objections and how to do so.

If your prospects have not raised any objections, you can encourage them by asking questions like:

→ What would stop an organisation like yours having a supplier like us?

→ Who looks after your current requirements?

→ So, would you be happy to proceed to the next step?

Timescale?

'Do I know precisely on what date my prospect intends to buy?'

This is probably the main area in which salespeople consistently misjudge. Yet, with a few simple and specific steps, they can quickly build up the quality of their sales pipeline. The dreaded words for a salesperson are usually when clients indicate that they are currently not in the market for anything that you are providing. The reasons may include:

→ We cannot get rid of the current stock

→ The budgets have been slashed

→ We have just signed a two year contract with your competitors

→ We have just purchased that

→ We're not interested

This is a difficult moment for most salespeople as they think of the time and effort to get this face-to-face meeting and the fact that, for the immediate future and for this month's figures anyway, they have completely wasted their time. No immediate sales benefits are going to accrue. A lot of salespeople usually politely, say: "thanks for giving me your time I will call you next month/year" as they meekly retreat, crushed with disappointment.

When prospects indicate to you that they are not currently in the market, try and have a strategic conversation with them and work on developing a strong relationship. Find out when they are likely to be in the market again. Too many salespeople work to their own selling cycles and not to those of their prospects.

For example, if prospects say that they have signed with another supplier until the end of the year, ask "can you please tell me what you think will be important to you and your organisation next year?" This approach gives you a chance of collecting information which, if you record it, diary it properly and most importantly, act on it, will give you a chance of getting a sale the next time. You will be calling at the right time thereby improving your odds.

Key Point

If you have missed a sales opportunity:

- find out when the prospects could be in the market again
- focus on building a relationship with them
- have a more strategic conversation
- record the information properly
- diary a call; AND
- act on it.

Establish time-related facts.

Solution and Size?

The salesperson should ask themselves:

→ Do I have the solution that the customer is looking for?

→ Is the type and size of this opportunity right for our organisation?

It's a 'yes' or a 'no.' It means that you have met the clients and understand exactly what they are looking for in terms of specification and pricing. It also means that you have established that the deal is not too big or too small and is right for your organisation.

Key Point

When it comes to Size, one must question as follows:

- Am I wasting my time working on this size of deal?
- Is this deal too small?

If it is, then pass on it.

- Is this a big opportunity?

If it is, then bring your manager in early in the sales cycle.

Using C MAGNETS for Sales Success

Under each of the elements of C MAGNETS, the crucial qualifying questions are identified. The answers to these questions are binary — either YES or NO. If the answer is Yes, you score 1 and No, you score 0. Unless you receive a definitive answer, the score should be taken as 0.

Scoring C MAGNETS

If, having received answers to all the qualifying questions, you have a score of five or less and cannot realistically address the current gaps (zeros) then you have no right to quote for the business. Your competition is in a stronger place and you are wasting your time and efforts. Qualify out of the opportunity as soon and as smoothly as possible, and do not chase after it. Invest your valuable

time more wisely elsewhere.

If you have a score of five or more and you can turn the zeros into ones then continue to qualify.

A score of seven is the minimum before you decide to qualify in. This means that you are going to give your all to win the business, it's currently the best use of your time and the odds of you winning increase, as your score increases.

If a diligent approach is taken to qualifying prospects, a salesperson will quickly establish the quality of their pipeline, thereby, increasing their chances of success.

Elements	Score
Competition?	0 or 1
Money?	0 or 1
Authority?	0 or 1
Goals?	0 or 1
Needs?	0 or 1
Encourage Objections?	0 or 1
Timescale?	0 or 1
Solution & Size?	0 or 1
TOTAL	

Obviously, the zero scores are the gaps that the salesperson needs to address with prospects. A salesperson should be able to establish all eight factors in a maximum of two face-to-face meetings.

How and When to Use C MAGNETS

The best time to use C MAGNETS is all the time during the sales process i.e. before, during and after meeting the prospect.

Before the meeting you may have some knowledge about an opportunity. By referring to C MAGNETS, it will allow you to prepare a specific question e.g. you might ask "How are new orders with new suppliers normally processed in your organisation?" to enquire about authority.

During the meeting, having C MAGNETS written across the top of your notes page can also help you in terms of an informal agenda for the meeting. Make sure you do not sound like you are going through a checklist.

After a first meeting it is a good investment to score the answer to the questions. The remaining 'zeros' will force you to ask yourself some questions:

→ Did I get the answer to that question?

- If no, then ask yourself — Do I need to get an answer before qualifying in and committing investment to the sales process?

- If yes, then ask yourself — Do I need to qualify out, say 'No', and invest resources elsewhere?

This is a sales tool that will help you, the salesperson, to find out what is the best use of your time. With the correct application, this tool will help you make more money, and reduce wasted time and effort. Guaranteed!

Summary of Chapter 4

→ C-MAGNETS will help you make the best use of your precious sales time

→ Always qualify your prospects rigourously

→ Early 'NOs' save you time

→ The C-MAGNETS qualifying tool should be used before, during and after the sales call

→ C-MAGNETS will make you more commission and save you time and effort

45

5 Influencing Skills

Chapter outline
Influencing Skills

→ Knowing Your Objectives
→ Managing Your Credibility
→ Watching Your Body Language and
  Personal Appearance
→ Negotiating Effectively

Influencing is an essential skill. No matter what you do in life, being able to influence the opinions and decisions of people, will have very beneficial outcomes. This is especially true if you find yourself in an organisation where sales is your primary responsibility. Here we will look at influencing from a *'sales effectiveness'* perspective.

A deep understanding and competence in the following four areas will enable you to become more influential.

Knowing Your Objectives

One of the fundamental habits recommended for all salespeople — novices and established salespeople alike — is to be very clear about your objectives prior to presenting yourself to your customer or prospect. By far the best way to achieve this is to write them down prior to the actual call. This will give your sales call a great sense of purpose and focus. It will also have the added benefit of making you more tenacious and professional if the meeting does not go according to plan. You should think and plan with only three key objectives in mind, otherwise you may lose focus. Having only three, sharpens the senses and priorities.

From the objectives below, choose the most important three and focus on them. Ask yourself:

→ Am I information gathering?

→ Am I looking for the prospect to take a particular action?

→ Am I looking to gain agreement on the next step forward?

→ Am I looking to be introduced to another person in the organisation?

→ Am I looking to upsell, cross sell, add another product line or get more shelf space?

→ Do I need to get a set of accounts?

→ Do I need to get them to agree a timescale for delivery?

→ What are my customers'/ prospects' personal priorities?

→ Why are they delaying the decision?

→ Who influences their careers?

A salesperson has much to do on any given sales call — focusing on a salesperson's objectives gives that call a better chance of being as productive as possible. Again, this can be easily achieved, if the salesperson takes the trouble to ask themselves:

→ What are the top three objectives in this call?

Key Point

Write down your top three objectives before your sales meeting and it will increase your chance of getting that sale.

Bear in mind, however, that many meetings do not go according to plan and be ready to let the meeting take its natural course. Be careful not to let your preconceived ideas dominate the meeting.

Unfortunately, observations of salespeople conducting calls tend to show that, rather than professionally planning their sales calls in advance, they leave it until the last minute. They often arrive under time pressure, dash in to the premises, and only start to think more deeply about the call while they are waiting for the prospect. This means that they are usually unprepared for the more difficult topics so they will try and avoid these on the call or revert to the over-used response *'I will come back to you on that.'*

This is a waste of time compared to the true sales professionals who will:

→ have done their homework

→ be clear about the main objectives of the meeting

→ have anticipated the most likely objections and

→ be prepared to add value to the meeting

These preparations, of course, do not guarantee the sale, but they do give the professional salesperson the best possible chance of winning it.

Managing Your Credibility

Buyers tend to make judgements on three levels:

→ your organisation

→ your team within that organisation

→ you personally

Remember that any interaction between a customer or prospect and an organisation is a *'moment of truth.'* So, a meeting is 'a moment of truth', an opportunity to prove that you will provide the best solution to your prospect's situation.

A happy customer has a habit of buying more products/services. Whether you are selling french fries or computers, the same underlying principles apply — happy customers buy more. This basic business philosophy makes it imperative that the sales professional understands how to meet and exceed customers' and prospects' expectations.

Credibility at an organisational, team and personal level can take a long time to establish, but literally seconds to lose. Your hard-earned credibility can even be lost over minor matters. All you need to do is set an expectation with a customer or prospect and then fail to deliver on it.

Key Point

The simple lesson here for the humble salesperson is:

Never, ever promise what you cannot deliver!

The advanced lesson is:

Always set an expectation that you can beat.

The key is:

Manage your credibility.

Many salespeople set an expectation that they fail to deliver on. Many sales calls finish 'I will get back to you first thing tomorrow with the answer to that.' They often then run into unforeseen difficulties and cannot deliver, thereby losing credibility.

Here is an alternative approach which is practical and simple – under promise and over deliver. If you do that during the sales process your credibility will be enhanced and you will get repeat business.

There is a really simple way to do that: instead of promising to get back as soon as possible, indicate to the prospect:

→ I will get back to you by close of business tomorrow, are you ok with that?

Typically, the prospect will agree to this. If the salesperson can get back to the prospect before lunch time the next day, then you have beaten the deadline and this clearly signals to the prospect that:

→ you were listening

→ you understand

→ you are timely

→ you care about them and their organisation

→ you are different from other salespeople

Consequently your credibility is enhanced.

Salespeople have so many opportunities to set expectations with a customer and then beat them. The sales professionals that consistently employ this method will have many happy customers who are delighted to give them repeat business.

Watching Your Body Language and Personal Appearance

It sounds so simple, but many so-called sales professionals do not have any understanding of how much of their one-to-one communication is expressed through their body language and personal appearance. Not that your personal appearance should be the dominant factor in whether you get the sale or not, but your personal appearance says a lot about what you think of yourself, the organisation you represent and the product that you sell. It also communicates to prospective customers what you think of them.

There are no excuses acceptable for not having immaculate:

→ Finger nails

→ Shoes

→ Hair

→ Suits

→ Shirts or blouses

→ Ties

The most important factor is the appropriateness of the clothing.

Your body language is even more important. According to Albert Mehrabian — Professor Emeritus of Psychology, UCLA, one of the most quoted authorities on human communication — when a person is unsure of your message, as much as:

→ 55% of your message will be conveyed by your body language;

→ 38% by the tone that you use; and,

→ only 7% by your actual words.

Professor Mehrabian was specifically referring to a person conveying their feelings or attitudes. So, the salesperson must be acutely aware of the importance of having harmony between their words, their tone and their body language. We are not looking for superman or superwoman here; just a salesperson who is professional, prepared, relaxed, credible and in control of his/her emotions and voice.

With regard to body language, you can, with practice and preparation, develop a frame of mind and the appropriate body language to deliver optimum performance.

Salespeople must be acutely aware of the importance of having harmony between their words, their tone and their body language.

Negotiating Effectively

Best Alternative To a Negotiated Agreement - BATNA

When it comes to negotiating homework, it is always a good idea to start with the end game in mind and then work your way through the process to get ready for the five different stages of negotiation:

→ Preparation

→ Understanding the other party

→ Clarifying your position

→ Seeking common ground

→ Closing

Figure out exactly what is *'your best alternative to a negotiated agreement'.*

BATNA was developed by negotiation researchers Roger Fisher and William Ury of the Harvard Program on Negotiation ("Getting to Yes", 1991).

In negotiations, the *'Best Alternative to A Negotiated Agreement'* or BATNA is the course of action that will be taken by you if the current sales negotiations fail. Effectively it is the plan B. It is advisable to give plan B a lot of consideration during the preparation phase. Understanding your BATNA should be a key driver in the negotiation process.

Panel 5.1

The 5 Stages of Negotiation

The 5 Stages of Negotiation

Preparation — 1

Understanding Others — 2

Clarifying Your Position — 3

Seeking Common Ground — 4

Closing — 5

In terms of your preparation for the sales negotiation it pays to understand what points/terms you are happy to change/concede. Understanding the precise point that you need to walk away from an opportunity is vital.

Preparation, as with so many skills, heavily influences the outcome of a negotiation. The saying *'proper planning and preparation prevents poor performance'* sounds like it was purpose-designed for negotiating. We should seek answers to Who? What? Where? Why? When? and How? in advance.

Understanding the other party will be easier if you employ the listening and questioning skills discussed in chapters 2 and 3. Knowing the motivation factors of the individuals/teams concerned will also help you to position your offering.

Clarifying your own position is best done by keeping your points simple and therefore easier to understand. Seeking the middle ground gives both parties a solid foundation upon which to go forward to the next stage of agreement.

Closing to final agreement takes patience and persistence from a sales perspective. You cannot close a complex sales opportunity without revisiting the five stages regularly. Some stages will need to be revisited as the needs and wants of both parties change during the sales process.

Fisher and Ury highlight the two different types of negotiating in their book, *'Getting to Yes'*:

Integrative negotiations are those where parties are seeking a 'Win/Win' resolution where both parties are satisfied with the outcome. They refer to this as *'growing the pie.'* On the other hand,

Distributive negotiations seek to *'divide the pie',* where one party wins and the other loses.

In the context of sales, it is important to understand that an integrative approach is preferable as it promotes trust and longer lasting relationships. It should also be understood that sometimes a distributive approach is selected by one of the parties.

Set out below are sales negotiating tips for both the *'once off sales'* and the regular *'business as usual'* sales calls.

'Once off sales' tips:

→ Always allow the buyer and recommender look good during the process, particularly in front of their bosses

→ Use assertive behaviour, focus on the result without hurting the other person

→ It must be win-win — benefitting both the salesperson and the prospect — if it's a deal that's going to stick and last

→ When seeking common ground, start by agreeing on all the things that you have agreed on; cementing the current position, before you go on to tackle new issues

→ Understand their personal motivation (fear of making a mistake or individual, team or organisational motivation)

→ Be prepared to say 'No, sorry we cannot do that'

→ Be ready to justify differences between your offering and your competition

→ Have a plan B. Know your BATNA

In relation to day-to-day regular sales calls made by key account managers or novice salespeople in whatever industry you are in, there is a very simple and sacrosanct rule.

Key Point

Ask yourself during the **preparation** phase of the call 'What are the three questions that I do not want to be asked during this call?'

If you can sincerely do your home work around these three areas,

53

then your level of confidence will be very high going into the call. This will allow you to have a lot more meaningful calls than the competitor who may drop in ill-prepared, hoping these issues do not come up during the call and who will respond in the utterly predictable line of 'I will get back to you on that.' To me, that is another *'moment of truth',* clearly signalling to the buyer whether you have or have not done your homework. Talk to your manager before the call if you require input and advice on important issues, it's much more professional and allows you to demonstrate that you are the best alternative.

Effective sales negotiations, big and small, are about doing your homework in advance of the call, not during or after. When it comes to winning over new customers, in a like-for-like competition, the sales professional with the most useful information usually wins.

Summary of Chapter 5

→ Have very clear objectives and write them down in advance of meetings

→ Manage and protect your credibility

→ Enhance your credibility by 'under-promising' and 'over-delivering'

→ Pay close attention to your body language and personal appearance

→ Understand the five different stages of negotiations and use these effectively in both big-ticket and smaller deals

→ Before every meeting, ask yourself "What are the three questions I do not want to be asked?" Do your homework!

→ Have a Plan B!

Objection Handling Skills

6

Chapter outline
Objection Handling Skills

→ Handling Objections Effectively
→ The *Feel, Felt, Found* Technique of
   Handling Objections and Beyond
→ Over 500 Scripts to Handle an Objection
→ Clarifying and Deepening Your
   Understanding of the Prospect

Handling Objections Effectively

The ability to handle objections effectively is very much at the heart and soul of effective selling. Professional salespeople will see objections from prospects and customers as an opportunity to prove that they and their company provide the best solutions.

Handling prospects' objections is simply part of the process of closing a sales opportunity. As a professional salesperson — if you have done your homework — you should relish the opportunity to discuss and respond to objections from the prospect. The more objections that you overcome, the closer you get to closing the sales opportunity.

Handling objections is not an adversarial exercise or encounter. Traditionally, it was deemed that the 'smart' salesperson must know more than the prospect and that the self-serving, high pressure salesperson would try to pull one over on the consumer.

A more consultative approach to handling a prospect's objections will be more productive. Consultation requires the prospect and the salesperson to sit down and discuss the objection together. This should result in a mutual decision being reached on the best solution to the prospect's problem.

Key Point
Objections are buying signals.

The sales transaction with 'No objections'

If a prospect has no objections for a salesperson during a meeting then the salesperson is being processed by the prospect. The prospect has no intention of buying but might actually be looking for free information and/or consultation from the seller. *'Give me as much information as you can because I want to bargain with another supplier'* is the mentality of this purchaser. It is a rare type of purchaser who has no objections.

The ability to handle objections effectively is very much at the heart and soul of effective selling.

Anticipating the objections

One of the cornerstones of successful selling is to plan and anticipate the objections that you might receive. Next, develop a selection of razor-sharp scripts that address these objections from the prospect's perspective, but be sure to use your active listening skills to first understand the **detail** of the objection.

The prospect is only likely to have a limited number of objections. The true professional will have a deep reservoir of quality responses to overcome these objections. The ability to handle objections well separates the champions from the also-rans in selling. The winners execute this particular process with aplomb. They handle objections naturally and with consummate ease, thereby reassuring the cautious decision maker. This skill is acquired with perseverance in the areas of research, prospect orientation and practice.

The professional salesperson will always see objections as a buying signal and act accordingly. If a prospect expresses an objection, it opens the door to further understanding and positioning on your part. It gives you the best chance of satisfying your prospect's needs and building an excellent future customer relationship.

Prospects usually object with a view to seeking more information or clarifying the information that they already have. This signals the start of the bargaining process.

The *Feel, Felt, Found* Technique of Handling Objections and Beyond

The following is a suggested framework to enable you to handle and overcome objections. Use these suggestions but ultimately, you should understand the objection handling process and develop your own scripts using your own industry language, as appropriate. The written word is a lot different from the spoken word. So the tone, pitch, pace and emphasis, not to mention body language, all play an important part in framing your response to objections and ultimately your sales success. The good news is that objections are very predictable, and, therefore, with the proper knowledge, skill, practice and attitude, easy to overcome.

> Winners execute this particular process with aplomb. They handle objections naturally and with consummate ease, thereby reassuring the cautious decision maker. This skill is acquired with perseverance in the areas of research, prospect orientation and practice.

Feel, Felt, Found, is a proven technique for handling objections. The professional salesperson should look to go well beyond the *Feel, Felt, Found,* script and handle with skill and empathy the important issues for prospects – who are, after all, future customers. This is a vital skill for individual, team and organisational success. If you execute this core one-to-one selling skill better than anybody in the market place you will be more successful.

The framework and principles that you will use are exactly the same as *Feel, Felt, Found.* Namely, objections are handled with only the prospects in mind. You respond only with their issues in mind. Your organisation's capabilities should only be mentioned if they can be translated directly into a benefit for a prospect. Your orientation in response to the objection should always be focused on the prospect, your future customer.

Approach

It is important when approaching people to be yourself, but be the best 'you' possible. **What you say is important but how** you say it **is more** important - hence the significance of prepared phraseology, both written and spoken. However, if you sound rehearsed, your prospects may feel that they are just another number to you and your credibility will suffer. It takes a professional salesperson to be able to handle routine objections and yet not sound rehearsed.

There are three stages in the *Feel, Felt, Found,* technique as outlined below.

> What you say is important but how you say it is more important.

STAGES	BASIC PHRASE	PURPOSE
FEEL	I/We understand how **you** feel.	Tunes in to what **the prospect** is saying not what you are thinking!
FELT	Other customers/ prospects (like **you**) felt the same way.	Acknowledges and validates **the prospect's** viewpoint and makes him/her feel more comfortable.
FOUND	They (prospects like **you**) found that our solution was much more competitive.	Demonstrates that other prospects have been on the same decision journey as **your prospect** and are now happy.

Over 500 Scripts to Handle an Objection

The mix of the combinations below represent over 500 separate ways to handle objections. You need to 'practise' to find out WHICH COMBINATION suits the prospect and you the best, in any objection situation.

A TOOL BOX FOR HANDLING OBJECTIONS	
Feel	I understand how **you** feel.
	Some other options; • I understand **you**. • I hear what **you** are saying. • **You're** not the first person to say that. • That's understandable from **your** perspective. • I see where you are coming from. • I appreciate what **you** are saying. • That's been mentioned before. • That's a point that is raised regularly.
Felt	We have a lot of customers on our books now who felt the same way.
	Some other options; • We have a lot of **customers who** expressed the same reservations as **you**. • Other **customers have** said that before. • Their concerns were identical to **yours**. • Our existing **customers?** Well, they were just like **you** now. • We have **customers who** expressed the same concerns. • Other customers **flagged** that to us before they signed with us.
Found	They found that our solution fixed their problem.
	Some other options; • **They** realised... • **They** have discovered... • **They** have seen, first hand the benefits/improvements. • **They** noticed... • **They** picked up on... • **They** now see how... • **They** have confirmed...

Key Point

Perfect practice makes perfect and permanent!

Clarifying and Deepening Your Understanding of the Prospect

Professional salespeople will always also use open questions to clarify with their customers/prospects: *"What do you mean by...?" "Please explain to me?" "Am I right in saying...?"* so that they deepen their understanding of their motivations. This is called *'Prescriptive Selling'* because, as with the doctor discussed earlier, a value-adding expert salesperson will seek to *'diagnose'* the prospect first in order to be better able to *'prescribe'* the best solution to *'fix'* the prospect's problem. The buyer values the salesperson's industry expertise and opinion. In this way, a deeper, longer-lasting buyer-seller relationship will be built.

Top Tips for Handling Objections:

Be Sure to:

> Check your own understanding through open questions
>
> - Know the most frequent and difficult objections
>
> - Understand these from the prospects' perspectives and what motivates them
>
> - Build up your reservoir of responses
>
> - Check your responses have a prospect orientation

Avoid:

> - Jumping in too quickly
>
> - Sounding rehearsed, it will only make you sound insincere

Actively Listen:

> - Actively listening is the best approach to ensure that you understand the objections
>
> - Look for the true meaning — sometimes there is more to the objection than first meets the eye

Wait until your prospect is completely finished:

> - Let the prospects give their full opinion — do not second guess them
>
> - Listen with intent - be seen to listen

Ask them to clarify:

- Please explain that fully to me
- What do you mean, not competitive?

Seek to understand:

- Is that your only concern?
- Use layering responses and questions to clarify

Justify and explain:

- Think *Feel, Felt, Found*
- Go beyond *Feel, Felt, Found*

Close to the next stage in the sales cycle:

- Get into their diary
- Get agreement on the decision, action and date

Summary of Chapter 6

→ Anticipate all possible objections

→ Have well-developed scripts to answer them

→ Make sure you do not sound rehearsed and that the responses have a customer orientation

→ Use *Feel, Felt, Found* and beyond

→ Clarify objections and deepen your understanding of your prospect

Closing Skills

7

Chapter outline
Closing Skills

→   The Elemental Sales Skill of Closing
→   Eight Different Closing Techniques

The Elemental Sales Skill of Closing

Closing skills in sales are akin to goals or points scored in sport — without them, you cannot have a decisive result. Closing skills are one of the key skills of the successful sales professional. Despite their importance, most salespeople learn closing skills informally 'on the job', by observing a colleague. This can be a defining moment in salespeople's careers as the closing skills that they pick up may or may not be the most suitable for the products/services or prospects/customers that they are dealing with.

ABC — Always Be Closing is a very cheesy, old sales cliché, that was immortalised by the performance of Alec Baldwin, playing the role of an aggressive Sales Manager in the film Glengarry Glenross. That said. *'always be closing'* has survived the test of time.

From a selling perspective, *'closing'* is defined as getting to the next stage in the sales process. Anywhere in the commercial continuum from researching the market to the customer's initial cheque clearing in the bank involves the skill of closing. Professional selling is a process where the ability to close effectively, clearly marks out the winners from the 'also-rans'.

Most salespeople do not actively close to the next stage of the sales process. They 'hope' that the prospect will drive the process. What they are actually doing is avoiding the possibility of a 'No'. By not asking for the business or looking to get agreement from the prospect to go to the next stage in the selling process, you damage your chances of getting a sale. It is another 'moment of truth', the opportunity to prove that you are the best alternative.

If the salesperson does not try to close to the next stage in the process, the prospect is often left with negative feelings — *"The salesperson has bigger fish to fry, I must be just a small opportunity, so he/she doesn't really care."* This is the last message that a salesperson wants to communicate. It is very important to ensure that you do not inadvertently lead your prospects to believe that they are unimportant to you and your organisation. Always ask for the business or get agreement to proceed to the next stage or suffer the consequences.

Key Point

Always **ASK** your prospect for permission to go the next stage.

Eight Different Closing Techniques

→ Alternative Close

→ Cautious Close (The Cautionary Tale)

→ Bargaining Close

→ Reference Close

→ Direct Close

→ Summary Close

→ Assumptive Close

→ Isolation Close

The Alternative Close is based upon the principle of offering the prospects only two options and asking them which one they would prefer. This could happen at the prospecting stage or the final signature stage.

- Would you be happy to meet on Friday morning or afternoon?

- Do you want to go ahead with option 1 or would you prefer option 2?

It is very useful when the client has been given a range of options to consider, for example the option to pay monthly, quarterly, half yearly or annually. The professional 'closer' will look to establish which of the options is the client least interested in and then focus on the final two.

Often, using the Alternative Close skilfully can bring greater clarity to the selling situation. The Alternative Closing method is also sometimes called the Either-Or-Close.

The Cautious Close (or The Cautionary Tale as it is sometimes known) is normally used to bring a small element of fear, uncertainty or doubt to a sales situation and thereby stimulate the prospect into agreeing to the next step. If the client acts or agrees now, then there will be a particular benefit accruing as a result of that action or decision

- If you sign now, we can guarantee the rate agreed.

- If we get the order by Friday we will deliver before the end of the month.

The key focus area for the professional salesperson is that the factor introduced must be outside of their control and it must be in the interest of the client to agree or act now.

- We currently have that product in stock, but there is a big demand for it. If you order now, you won't be disappointed.

The Bargaining Close is another basic closing method and is strictly about giving to receive.

- If I can reduce the price, will you sign the order now?

- I can give you a better price if you commit to a larger quantity.

Salespeople should never give anything away without receiving something in return or else they will lose credibility. If a salesperson revisits a prospect with news of a price cut, the prospect is likely to question why the price was so high in the first place. This may encourage the prospect to feel that the initial price was a 'try on.'

Bargaining is about giving so that you will receive.

This type of 'close' is often used when the seller and/or the buyer are approaching deadlines.

The Reference Close is all about giving the prospect the comfort that you are able to deliver for them. Often the salesperson will sell themselves and the product but will forget to sell the company. This is a particular challenge for small to medium sized enterprises who sell to larger, more established organisations who rate reliability high on their shopping list. For the smaller sized companies, it

is recommended that you use the names (and testimonials if possible) of those with whom you have done business in order to make your sale.

> 'By my customers you shall know me.'

This is a very good principle. If you have customers who are better known and more widely recognised than your own company's brand, then position these reference customers with your new prospects (making sure that you have your customer's permission first).

- Yes, we may be small, but that has not stoppped us from doing business with IBM.

- We have delivered projects in other Government Departments.

The use of independent third party public commentaries like newspapers, industry awards and magazine articles is highly recommended, where possible. These comments can really help you close sales opportunities to the next stage.

- It's true, we are small, but we have been featured in the press, winning an industry award from X as an innovative organisation.

This close is most suitable when the prospect trusts you and is happy with your product/service but is not quite sure about your

67

organisation, because they may not have heard of it.

The Direct Close is simplicity in selling.

- Would you like to place that order now?

- So, in principle, you are happy to proceed?

It is so effective, it hardly needs explanation. If it does not work the first time then the prospect may have an objection. The professional salesperson will be prepared to handle this. It is interesting to note that many salespeople feel that this can be a very blunt way to close and are not that comfortable with it. Try it, when appropriate. It is very reliable.

The Summary Close should be used when the salesperson is summarising a conversation or a presentation and is looking for agreement to go to the next stage in the sales process. It is very useful because:

- It can be dropped into a conversation at any time

- It clearly signals to the buyer that you are looking for their agreement to get to the next step

- It gives the buyer time to think of objections and thereby gives you the opportunity to deal with them

- It gives you a chance to show the buyers that you have clearly listened to them

- It is a 'gentle' close and is in no way pushy or threatening to the buyer

You may find the following suitable for use with your prospects:

- Do you mind if I just summarise where we are at with a view to agreeing the next steps?

- Do you think a review with a view to deciding the next steps would be useful at this stage?

Salespeople should select language with which they are comfortable. If you are not comfortable with the wording of the above examples, adapt them and practise using the correct pace, tone and emphasis. It is important to emphasise that the use of closing techniques allows you to extract objections from a prospect, thereby giving you a chance to deal with them.

Key Point

The 'faint-hearted' salesperson hopes that the prospect does not have any objections while the true sales professional welcomes the chance to deal with any objections up front and move to the next stage.

This type of 'close' is most useful when there are a lot of variables in the sale, such as different products/services, a variety of delivery locations and a number of people involved. It is most suitable when taking a *'consultative'* approach to closing the sale.

The Assumptive Close is definitely the 'close' that brings to mind aggressive 'door-to-door' salespeople, shady car salespeople and double glazing sales mercenaries who may be trying to get one over on the customer.

This type of close has a wide range of applications, but, as the name 'Assumptive' suggests, the underlying philosophy is that you assume that you are getting the sale. Used in the right way, it can be a powerful closing technique. It can be gentle or aggressive. What is most important is that it is great for getting results or generating further objections that you can deal with.

A subtle application may be:

- Will I book those dates in the diary now?

A more extreme application, is arriving to the meeting with a pre-filled purchase order and asking the prospect:

- Would you mind authorising the order?

It can be dangerous too, so good judgement and skill are required as to when and how to use it. Despite this, when used properly, it allows you to find out where you stand with the prospect and you can trim your sail accordingly.

You could be told *'We are not at that stage yet,'* which allows you to gently enquire *'Can you please tell me exactly what stage we are at?'*

This type of probing question must be asked the right way. Your attitude, tone, pace, emphasis and volume are even more important than the words you use.

A combination of the assumptive 'close' and the 'diary' works well when trying to get a meeting.

- How does early Friday afternoon next week suit you?

- Shall we put a couple of provisional dates in the diary at this stage?

When using this technique, be prepared for objections — if they are not ready to agree to go to the next step in the sales process, they will have objections. As a professional salesperson, you want to know exactly what the objections are so that you can deal with them.

The Isolation Close is most appropriate when dealing with the adversarial buyer who is either trained to, or, instinctively wants to bring salespeople to their knees. This adversarial buyer has been known to play with salespeople for sport. They are not that fond of salespeople and usually do not trust or like them. Typically, this competitive foe will not be satisfied until they hear the salesperson say 'No' or 'I am sorry, I cannot do that' (usually reduce the price more). So hearing 'No' from the salesperson is a very important part of their buying process.

Typically, the diplomatic salesperson will be looking to please the buyer as much as possible. Every time the salesperson is about to close, the buyer will have another problem. This over-eager salesperson will once again go back to the office, get their boss involved, re-negotiate the deal and finally present a new solution to the competitive buyer. What is guaranteed is that the buyer will have another problem for the seller.

If our sales professionals were armed with the following phrases, then, they could save themselves and their organisations a lot of misspent effort.

- If I fix that, will you then go ahead?

- If that's sorted, will you give us the order?

- If we remedy that situation, will you issue the purchase order?

Strong eye contact is important for the isolation close. This takes the commitment to a very personal level.

If our sales professionals were armed with the above phrases, then, they could save themselves and their organisations a lot of misspent effort.

Key Point

Try the different closing techniques — different techniques will suit different situations.

Summary of Chapter 7

→ Always ASK your prospect for permission to go to the next stage

→ Welcome the opportunity to deal with objections

→ 'Always **Be** Closing' — during and at the end of sales meetings — to go to the next stage in the sales process

→ Eight *'closing techniques'* are like eight different tools; each one is designed to do a specific job

→ The right combinations, when used together, can really produce the right results

→ Understand the framework and the process and adapt the tools to your specific situation

→ Many salespeople understand the process and the tools, but often fail to sharpen them for their own use

→ The most skilful salespeople and sports people have a major common ground — they continually seek to improve their techniques and practise until the new skill becomes second nature

→ A sales specialist with eight different closing techniques (and multiple combinations of them in their arsenal) used judiciously, will be a potent force in the marketplace!

8

Four Winning Sales Habits

Chapter outline
Four Winning Sales Habits

→ Have a Call Plan for Every Sales Call
→ Systematically Improve your Sales Effectiveness by Reviewing the Call
→ Recognise Buyers' Personal Styles and Flex Your Own
→ Be Assertive During the Sales Process

The skils outlined in this chapter are not core sales skills but are the icing on the cake that allow you to go the extra mile in pursuit of sales success. They are like the other half of a double act that together is more memorable. Think of the following combinations: Bread and butter, Apple pie and cream and Laurel and Hardy. Just like the core selling skills, the separate stars **can** stand alone, but when paired with the right partners, the impact is very effective. The following tool, tip and skill are the extras that you should understand and develop to partner with your core selling skills.

Have a Call Plan for Every Sales Call

The one factor that separates the successful salespeople from the pack is the level of preparation that they do in advance of a sales call whether they are meeting a prospect or an existing customer. This is a *clear indicator* of professionalism. Many face-to-face salespeople arrive for a meeting under time pressure.

Upon arrival, usually while they are waiting for their contact to collect them at reception, the salesperson really starts thinking about the impending meeting. Sometimes, the buyers will not even notice this lack of preparedness as they have already decided that they are buying from the company that the salesperson represents. Alternatively, a tight marginal decision between two companies may be swayed by the more professional salesperson who prepares fully in advance of the sales meeting.

Key Point

Always have a call plan.

In terms of call plans for sales meetings, the following approach is recommended. If you have the precision and discipline to execute this process, you will be more successful. The following questions are worthy of consideration and commitment to paper well before you walk into the prospect's or customer's premises.

Just Ask Yourself:

→ **What are the top three objectives of this call?**

- Write them down

- This will give you focus, determination and resilience in the face of objections

→ **What are the top three objections that I can anticipate?**

- Again, write them down

- One will be price

- Figure out the other two and have a response plan

- This process will give you more confidence when the objections are raised

→ **What are the three best/most important questions that I can ask the prospect?**

- Identify and write them down ahead of the meeting; this is a great investment

- This allows you to direct the conversation

- This will help you be different from the competition

- You can display your organisational, team and individual *'value add'*

- Get these questions right and you can show all important empathy

- It shows 'I/We understand you and can help you'

→ **Is my qualifying C MAGNETS score still valid or has this opportunity status changed?**

- Check the current qualifying score

- This helps highlight the areas that you need to focus on

→ **What and when is the next action agreed with the customer or prospect?**

- This is the acid test of your call

- What action have you jointly agreed and when is the date?

Systematically Improve Your Sales Effectiveness by Reviewing the Call

As you know, not all calls go according to plan. The following review will help you to accelerate up the sales learning curve. It will lead to effective change on your sales calls and will help you get better results.

Key Point

The work, learn, change review.

After the face-to-face call, every salesperson should ask:

- What worked on that call?

- What have I learned?

- If I was doing that call again, what would I change?

Having a sales call plan for every single call and completing a work, learn and change review, will give you a process that will quickly contribute to your success in sales.

Recognise Buyers' Personal Styles and Flex Your Own

There is very good and extensive literature written about individual personalities and styles. Understanding different personalities will help you in the sales process.

Sometimes you meet a new person such as a customer or colleague, and you know within the first few minutes — *'I am going to get along with this person.'* At the end of your first meeting, you find yourself looking forward to meeting them again. You are both 'on the same page', you really work well together and you feel that your job is more fulfilling as a result.

Then, there are some people, customers or colleagues who evoke the exact opposite feelings in you. You know after a short while, *'this is going to be hard work.'* Working with them is adversarial, draining and even disagreeable. You are glad that all your customers and colleagues are not like that person.

→ Why does this happen?

→ What do you do?

→ How do you deal with them?

Here are some pointers:

→ The most common characteristic that people share is that they are different

→ Different differences matter to different people

→ Underneath it all most of us want similar things:

- Survival, security, belonging, love, recognition, self-esteem, happiness

→ Acknowledging, recognising and dealing with different people are the keys to your success in selling

From a sales perspective, it is useful to understand that most people are a combination of *'thinkers'* and *'doers.'* Understanding the more dominant role in your new prospects/customers can give keys to 'exactly' how to deal with them.

Thinkers

'Thinkers' are typically:

- Information dependent, they need as much information as possible about your products/services

- Not excited by new information, they are called low reactors

- Capable of taking in and analysing a lot of information

- Desirous of certainty, facts, proof and detail

- Good at asking considered,

detailed and awkward questions

- Uncomfortable with vagueness, uncertainty, being first to try something

- Able to learn best by thinking and proving logical and rational outcomes

'Thinkers' like to think first then shoot!

Doers

'Doers' are typically:

- Comfortable with new ideas, uncertainty and mistakes

- Willing to try new things

- Quick to try things before thinking about them, action oriented

- Willing to try anything once

- One page people, who like summaries and, pictures if possible

- Able to learn best by doing and learning from their mistakes

'Doers' like to shoot first, then think!

How will I know a thinker from a doer?

The following is a general guide only and is based on my own use, over a ten year period of face-to-face selling in a business-to-business environment. Understand that, because human behaviour is involved, there will always be an exception to the following guidelines. That said, one way of helping to recognise a 'thinker' from a 'doer' is to be aware of their cadence. Cadence is simply the speed at which somebody naturally does something, such as:

- How quickly they walk

- How fast they talk

- How swiftly they eat

- The number of questions they ask as distinct from the depth of their considered questions

As you may expect, 'thinkers' and 'doers' generally do things at a different speed. The sooner you can recognise who you are dealing with, the quicker you can flex your own style.

Key Point

Flex your personal style relative to your interpretation of the other person.

The reason for flexing your own style is so that a deeper rapport can be built. If you do this, you have a better chance of getting the vital information you need to win the business.

The sooner you can recognise who you are dealing with, the quicker you can flex your own style.

Case Study

Background

I was selling training services to a large multinational. The procurement process was very formal. Vendors were instructed to just quote a daily price and a suggested agenda, no support material was the final instruction in the procurement website. They then selected four suppliers for an interview and same day final decision.

Situation

I was convinced the procurement executive was a 'doer'. A classic 'one page' type of person. Quick decisions, no detailed information and move quickly to the next stage in the process. However, I couldn't help thinking: 'What do I do if I'm wrong and the decision maker is the total opposite?' How do you quickly build rapport with a stranger in a selling environment?

Solution

As I sat in reception, I had one solution ready to be presented two different ways, in two different folders in my briefcase. One folder was tailor-made for the aforementioned 'doer'. A one-pager with a process diagram and suggested agenda. Perfect for a quick understanding and decision. The other folder had a lot of information, including examples of each presentation, together with some academic reading material. I also included a selection of papers that he may want to discuss on topics that could be included in the agenda.

As the decision maker walked towards me he was walking slowly, talking slowly and was armed with a folder full of paper. Before I got out of the chair I had a fair idea which one of my folders he would be getting. As we walked to the meeting room, and he asked me a very detailed question, I had to remind myself that I needed to slow my speech down and be prepared for more detailed questions. His eyes lit up when I produced all the information. Clearly, my competitors followed instructions. The purchaser was not happy, but it did not matter as he was not making the decision. We won the business.

Be Assertive During the Sales Process

Assertiveness is one of the key life skills, and a natural bedfellow for the consummate sales professional. It is defined as:

Standing up for your rights, needs and wants; in a way that respects the rights, needs and wants of others.

Unfortunately, being assertive is also widely misunderstood. Most people just implement the first part and 'stand up for their rights needs and wants' in an aggressive way, and completely miss the opportunity to get their result by being assertive.

Aggressiveness can be seen as 'attacking the person' whereas assertiveness 'addresses the issue.' Aggressive behaviour can manifest itself in the public domain when dissatisfied consumers 'give out' to staff in a restaurant in an aggressive way. What the complainer usually fails to recognise is that this person probably did not cause the problem but is very much the 'key' to resolving the issue. A better approach is to ask 'can you help me please?' This approach does not guarantee satisfaction but gives you the best chance of getting it.

Another way of defining assertiveness is:

'Focusing on getting the result without hurting others'.

OR

'Treating others exactly the way you would like to be treated'.

In the context of selling to prospects, customers, colleagues and team members, being assertive is about trying to really live up to the two challenges above. Again, no results are guaranteed, but it is energising to know that you have behaved appropriately and have given yourself every chance of getting the result.

Key Point

Treat others **exactly** the way you would like to be treated.

In the context of winning sales and dealing with the different types of characters that you meet in the course of your work, the ability to be assertive will serve you very well. It is very helpful when you encounter that small minority of people who treat salespeople in a less than helpful way. This type of person can be encountered in all walks of life. So, don't be surprised when you encounter them. These people are out there — being assertive and appropriate will protect you from their negative messages.

Summary of Chapter 8

→ Have a call plan for every single sales call

→ Use the work, learn, change and review approach to improve your sales effectiveness

→ Try to recognise the *'Thinker'* versus the *'Doer'*

→ Flex your personal style relative to your interpretation of the other person

→ Focus on getting results without hurting the other person

→ Treat others **exactly** the way you would like to be treated

Leading the Sales Team

9

Chapter outline
Leading the Sales Team

→ The Responsibilities of a Sales Manager
→ Sales Leadership Skills
→ Sales Recruitment
→ The Two Essential Sales Abilities
→ Managing the Sales Pipeline Stages
→ Tough Questions for Your Team

The Responsibilities of a Sales Manager

Henry Mintzberg in "The Nature of Managerial Work", 1973; defines the role of managers as:

> "Maximising the efficient use of scarce resources."

This quote captures the reality of sales management. Every month (the typical measurement cycle) you are very clearly judged by everyone in your organisation and by customers and prospects in your marketplace.

→ Did you make your number?

→ Did you hit your target?

→ Are you on track for the year?

→ Are we gaining market share?

The answers to these questions will determine whether or not you are viewed as a successful Sales Manager.

Among other things, a Sales Manager is responsible for:

→ Devising, executing and deploying sales strategy

→ Frontline activity, that crucial space between the prospect/customer and your sales team

→ Delivering a level of expected sales revenue within a time period. This revenue expectation is usually set in the context of the previous year's number and may have an expected level of growth

Your decisions directly impact the income and viability of your organisation. Despite this, you will find that you never have enough quality time, quality people, quality resources and/or quality prospects to reach your goals. In fact, a major challenge for salespeople and Sales Managers in particular, is effective time management – they often find themselves working on urgent, instead of, important matters.

Key Point

When you have a 'to do list' that seems overwhelming; answering the following question will give you a focus point for action.

'What exactly is the best use of my time right now?'

Sales Leadership Skills

Despite the importance of Sales Managers to organisations, they often don't have a strategy or a well thought-out plan to follow, never mind the possibility of a plan B or C to be used when market conditions change.

Convention dictates that well-organised Sales Managers will:

→ Plan

→ Lead

→ Organise, and

→ Control

the resources at their disposal. The planning, organising and controlling of resources are technical skills. These skills can be learned to a certain level of competence. The sales plan should be agreed in the context of the firm's overall strategy and specifically 'fit' with the marketing plan.

The skill of leading is vital for the long term success of a sales team. One core difference between management and leadership is the ability to inspire; to be able to motivate a person. Dwight Eisenhower captured it best when he said:

> "Leadership is the art of getting someone else to do something you want done because he wants to do it."

Sales leadership skills include persuading, influencing, understanding and inspiring individuals and teams to achieve the sales goals. This is different from making people do something. The telling and instructing Sales Manager is usually focused on the short term results. An effective Sales Manager is able to motivate people to achieve sales goals because they want to achieve them.

The key question is how? How do leaders create the willingness among other people to do something well? *'Pulling rather than pushing'* – as leadership gurus Warren Bennis and Burt Nanus describe in their book "Leaders", 1986. Having knowledge about, access to and skill in using motivation tools is important for long term success. The toolbox should include but not be limited to:

→ Approving, praising and recognising performance in public

→ Giving trust, granting respect and setting high expectations

→ Demonstrating loyalty so that it may be received

→ Removing organisational barriers that stand in the way of individual and team performances (smoothing processes, systems, access to resources)

→ Facilitating job enrichment, rotation and enlargement

→ Ensuring good communications across your team

→ Providing clear financial incentives

Only one of the above motivators relate directly to money. The other motivating tools require a longer term investment in relationships that most Sales Managers tend to put on the long finger.

Sales performance depends on the *competence* of the person, the *environment* they are in and individual *motivation*. A deficiency in any of these areas will hurt sales results. A sales leader must pay attention to all three areas. The key questions for the sales leader regarding the Sales Team and salespeople involved are:

→ Do they have the knowledge, skills and attitude to sell our products/services?

→ Have I provided the enabling conditions for the success of the sales team?

→ Are they motivated to sell?

Naturally, it is more helpful to clarify this at the sales recruitment stage.

Sales Recruitment

Recruitment is an inevitable part of a Sales Manager's job. Many expensive mistakes are made at this stage. A lot of quota-carrying managers can struggle to replace a departing but successful team member. So, the inexperienced manager recruits a new team member 'hoping' they will fit into the team. This road is fraught with danger.

> What makes successful salespeople?
>
> Are they born or are they made?
>
> How can I tell before I hire them?

The above questions are subject to the most intense debate. After years of research there is still no reliable way of predicting if your interview candidate will be a top sales producer. Despite its politically incorrect title, the Harvard Business Review article *"What Makes A Good Salesman"* by David Mayer and Herbert M. Greenberg (July-August 2006), raises some excellent points in relation to traditional recruitment and discusses two, seemingly incompatible, qualities that hiring managers should focus on in the hiring process — empathy with customers and the need to overcome the customer's hesitation to buy. Their basic theory is that a good salesperson must have at least two basic qualities: *empathy* and *ego drive*.

The Two Essential Sales Abilities

Empathy: the ability to feel; the central attribute that allows a salesperson to *'feel'* the way the prospect does, in order to sell them a product/service. This facilitates the key, and priceless, skill of getting powerful feedback from the prospect during the sales process. This helps salespeople have a customer orientation and enables them to be adaptable in presenting their solution.

Ego drive: the undeniable need to conquer in order to bolster one's self worth. This quality is a must-have for good salespeople.

> *"It makes them want, and need, to make the sale in a personal or ego way" Mayer & Greenberg.*

The chase and the conquest provide a powerful mechanism for self-esteem. Even losing a sale provides more motivation to go and get another sale.

With the salesperson's sensitive side *(empathy)* and intense need for winning *(ego)*, he/she can:

→ focus in on and understand, the motivating reason why the prospect is buying, and

→ target the offering more effectively and close the sale.

These salespeople have the competitive energy to go out and get the prospects and, using their empathy, the critical means to turn them into customers.

Key Point

Hire for the twin abilities of *Empathy* and *Ego drive.*

The next time you are interviewing a prospective candidate, it may be useful to view them in the context of *empathy* and *ego drive*. In fact, consider plotting those two variables into the following framework.

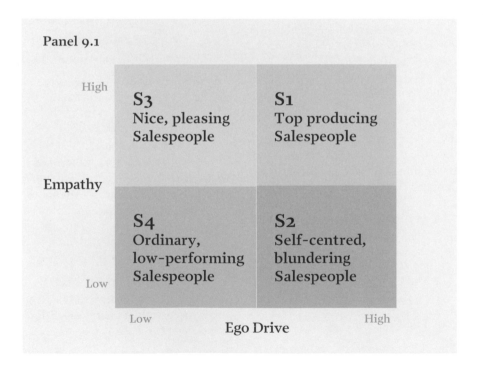

Panel 9.1

S3 Nice, pleasing Salespeople	**S1** Top producing Salespeople
S4 Ordinary, low-performing Salespeople	**S2** Self-centred, blundering Salespeople

High — Empathy — Low

Low — Ego Drive — High

If we look at the sales ability drivers of *Ego drive* and *Empathy*, we can have a wide range of combinations.

S1: High on Ego Drive and Empathy.

Your target for high performers. Salespeople in this quadrant have both qualities in abundance.

S2: Low on Empathy and High on Ego Drive.

Salespeople in this quadrant will typically blunder through the sales process hoping to hit the target. They can cause you and your organisation damage. They are mercenary in their approach to customers.

S3: High on Empathy and Low on Ego Drive.

This salesperson is 'nice'. Many long term salespeople reside here. They are sociable, presentable and diplomatic but lack the necessary drive to consistently close sales opportunities. They get hired because they 'fit' into the organisation and are liked, even though they often demonstrate low sales ability.

S4: Low on Empathy and Low on Ego Drive.

Mayer & Greenberg say that *"A salesman without much empathy or drive should not actually be a salesman, although a great many present salesmen fall into this group."*

Think of the amount of resources that you will waste trying to get employees to be successful salespeople if they 'don't have it in them' to be a sales producer.

Mayer & Greenberg's research insights will help you to at least target the right type of candidate, with the right core traits from which top sales producers are made.

They also claim that personality testing for top salespeople is an exercise in failure because *"The ability to sell, an exceedingly human and totally non-mechanical aptitude, has resisted attempts to measure it effectively."* The main reasons are:

→ Personality tests have been looking for interests not ability

→ People can fake test answers

→ Testing favours conformity, not individual creativity and leads to mediocrity

→ Tests have tried to isolate and measure some personality traits rather than reveal the whole dynamics of the person

Mayer & Greenberg claim that:

→ Sales ability is more important than sales experience

→ Sales ability is more important than the products being sold

→ Experienced recruits who have been head-hunted often do not work out

→ Companies need to seek more people with basic sales potential from a wider pool

testing for empathy and ego drive in an interview is challenging, but there may be clues in the candidate's deportment, attitude, listening and questioning skills, and track record. What is clear is that competent salespeople will have:

→ **Knowledge**

– the know-how to do the job.

→ **Skills**

– the abilities to do the job.

→ **Attitude**

– the 'way' they do the job.

John McInerney (Marketing & Sales Consultant) advises Sales Managers who are recruiting to:

> "Recruit for attitude and train for knowledge and skill as your sales will only ever be as good as the team you recruit."

There are many ways to test for these attributes, but the only real proof is in the actual sales results. Results don't lie but they give you feedback after you have made the decision to hire the candidate.

Key Point

The best defence against a wrong hiring decision is to have an on-going process of interviewing candidates.

Build a file of high potential recruits. This will give you a better prospect of hiring 'the one in ten' person who has top sales producer abilities. Try not to hire under pressure and do get other experienced managers involved in the crucial decision about "whether this candidate is really suitable to execute the sales strategy of your team?"

If you can raise your awareness about the importance of *empathy* and *ego drive*, the failure of personality testing, the importance of sales abilities, and the importance of attitude then the next hiring or firing decision that you make may be better.

Take responsibility for having the right 'people' on your Sales team.

Managing the Sales Pipeline Stages

Key Point

A sales pipeline is a range of qualified sales opportunities that are currently awaiting movement to a different stage in the pipeline.

Pipeline management and sales language are like music and dance; they come in so many different variations and guises. One of the key functions for a Sales Manager is to make sure the whole team and, indeed the company, understand the importance of having and using a single common sales language. This language must be fully understood in the context of managing the sales pipeline and can be used to specifically classify opportunities at each stage of the pipeline.

Most sales pipelines can be broken down into the following stages:

1. Addressable opportunities/leads

2. Contact made

3. Appointment agreed

4. Qualifying and information gathering

5. Qualifying in

6. Qualifying Out

7. Quotation given to customer

8. Awaiting decision

9. Verbal agreement 'yes'

10. Signed contract

11. Delivery of product/service

12. Payment received

Clear questions like:

→ Have you contacted that prospect?

→ Have you qualified that opportunity?

→ Have you agreed the next steps with the customer?

→ What stage is that opportunity at?

Panel 9.2

Typical Sales Pipeline Stages

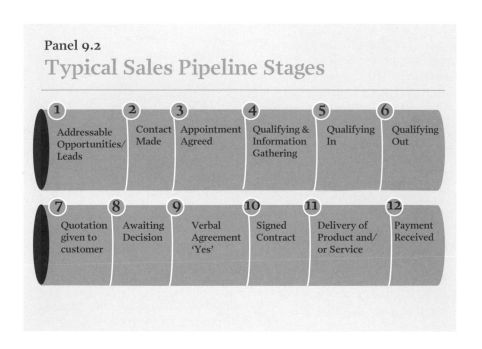

1	2	3	4	5	6
Addressable Opportunities/ Leads	Contact Made	Appointment Agreed	Qualifying & Information Gathering	Qualifying In	Qualifying Out

7	8	9	10	11	12
Quotation given to customer	Awaiting Decision	Verbal Agreement 'Yes'	Signed Contract	Delivery of Product and/ or Service	Payment Received

These questions are open to a wide range of answers. Clearly, defining the sales steps and definitions is crucial to effective communication in the team and across the organisation. This will bring clarity and purpose to managing sales pipelines.

If you take a 'black and white' view of the sales opportunities in your pipeline then you are starting on the right foot. Some rigour in this process will save a lot of headaches as a sales pipeline that is more robust in terms of depth and breadth will emerge. This process is about consistently identifying an accurate deal flow when managing and forecasting your sales revenue. This will result in more accurate sales forecasting.

If you work this process in a sales environment, you will quickly realise that *'hitting your target'* is a numbers game. The challenge is to make it a 'quality' numbers game.

Sales managers should ensure that their team members vigorously qualify the opportunities right through this whole process. If a salesperson concludes that the customer has no money after the first appointment, do not bother sending out a proposal. This just creates unnecessary noise in your organisation and is a waste of your precious resources. It is a numbers game, make sure that you at least work with well-qualified opportunities.

Key Point

The key to successfully hitting your target is:

The more qualified appointments your team have, the more qualified quotes they will send out and the more sales they will close.

Tough Questions for Your Team

Hard questions are very much part of a successful Sales Manager's tool-kit. The focus of the questions for your team is shown in the key point below:

Key Point

Asking a salesperson the following questions about an opportunity will give you immediate clarity:

- What action have you agreed with the prospect?
- When will this task happen?
- What is the intended outcome?
- How well is the opportunity qualified
- What is Plan B?

In a badly managed sales pipeline there is a lot of *'Noise'* i.e. opportunities that are never going to close. This hampers productivity in your organisation.

Good pipeline management is about minimising the *'Noise'* by removing these non-opportunities from your pipeline. This gives you a more realistic picture of qualified sales opportunities that are currently at different stages of the sales cycle. This will facilitate better forecasting and better deployment of the team's resources.

Pipelines should be used to manage the individual salespeople within your team. What will become clear from the configuration of the sales pipeline is where your team member is investing most of his/her time. It will also highlight what are the next action points for the salesperson. Often salespeople will have particular strengths, like cold calling, or closing, or proposal writing. These talents/ preferences are usually reflected in the shape of the pipeline.

Summary of Chapter 9

→ Plan, lead, organise and control the sales resources at your disposal

→ Always maximise the efficient use of scarce resources

→ A Sales Manager must provide the enabling conditions for the success of the sales team

→ The key characteristics of a successful salesperson are empathy and ego drive

→ Take responsibility for having

the 'right people' on your sales team

→ Have a common sales language that is understood by the whole team

→ Use pipelines to manage teams and individuals

→ Know the hard questions to ask a salesperson

10 Ronan's Selling Rules

Ronan's Selling Rules

Chapter One —
Developing New Business

→ Take responsibility and know your numbers

→ Sales pipelines do not lie! They tell you exactly where you are in relation to making your goals

→ Contact one new prospect every day!

→ If you are not out there you will not get there!

→ If you are in a numbers game, make it a quality numbers game

Chapter Two —
Listening Skills

→ Use your ears twice as much as your mouth

→ Listen with intent

→ Understand with empathy

→ Remember the 'coffee cup test'

Chapter Three —
Questioning Skills

→ Question with perception

→ The prospect is the best source of real, actionable information

→ 'HOW?' and 'WHAT?' are powerful questions

→ Prepare your three best/ most important questions in advance of meetings

Chapter Four —
Qualifying Skills

→ Early 'NOs' give you more time to succeed

→ Know what opportunities to walk away from

→ In a 50/50 decision, trust your gut - it's probably right

→ Learn! Learn more and know more than your competition

→ When you lose, learn and move on!

→ When you win, learn and don't forget!

Chapter Five —
Influencing Skills

→ Manage your credibility

→ Set expectations you can beat!

→ Motivate your prospects or customers to act by asking them to articulate the impact of either doing something OR not doing something e.g. 'What happens if your sales force are not properly trained?'

→ First Impressions COUNT — watch your body language and be appropriately groomed

Chapter Six —
Objection Handling Skills

→ Objections are buying signals

→ Expand your objection handling vocabulary

→ Go beyond *Feel, Felt, Found*

→ Perfect practice makes perfect and permanent

Chapter Seven –
Closing Skills

→ ASK for agreement to go to the next stage

→ Close with intention

→ Expand your closing vocabulary

→ Try different closing techniques

→ Always be closing both during and at the end of sales meetings

Chapter Eight –
Four Winning Sales Habits

→ Always have a call plan:

- What are the three questions that you do not want to be asked on this call? (N.B. do your homework on these)

- What are your three objectives for this call?

- What three questions can motivate my prospect to ACT?

- Systematically review the sales call

- What worked? What did you learn? What would you change?

→ Understand the personal style of the person to whom you are selling and flex your own

→ Treat others exactly the way you would like to be treated yourself

Chapter Nine –
Leading the Sales Team

→ Hire for the twin abilities of Empathy and Ego drive

→ Ask yourself regularly: 'What is the best use of my time right now?'

→ Have a Plan B

→ When there is no sales process, there is a problem

→ Understand what motivates the individuals on your team

> Stand out from the competition – be consistently professional!

Sales Calls

→ Be prepared!

→ Do your homework

→ Set and beat expectations

→ Never waste a call

→ Never ever lie to a prospect!

→ Never promise what you cannot deliver

→ Be different from your competitors!

→ Every interaction with a customer and prospect is an opportunity to prove that you are the best alternative

→ Ask yourself: What do my prospects need to do or say to convince their boss that they should pick your company?

Yourself

→ It's not what happens to you in selling that matters, rather your reaction to it

→ Develop and hone your selling skills

→ Expand your selling arsenal

→ Ask yourself every day 'What three actions can I take today to improve my sales performance?'

→ Learn something new every day – ask yourself 'What did I learn today?'

> Whatever you do in sales, sell to win!

Notes

Notes

Notes

Notes

Notes

Notes

Notes

Further publications in 2011 and 2012

- → Managing Reward
- → Handling Discipline - *Best Practice*
- → Managing Diversity
- → Negotiating Skills
- → Burnout
- → Coaching Skills
- → Life Balance
- → Conflict Resolution
- → Influencing Skills
- → Mediation Skills
- → Assertiveness and Self-Esteem
- → Strategic Issue Communications
- → Personal Development
- → Innovation
- → Compliance
- → Strategy Development and Implementation
- → Leadership and Strategic Change
- → Managing with Impact - *Focusing on Performance through People*
- → Strategic Marketing
- → Entrepreneurial Skills
- → Managing Attendance at Work
- → Employee Relations
- → Improving your Writing Skills
- → Organisation Development/ Training
- → Change Management
- → Organisation Design
- → Energy Management
- → International Marketing
- → Governance in Today's Corporate World
- → Customer Relationship Management
- → Building Commitment to Quality
- → Understanding Finance
- → PR Skills for Managers
- → Logistics and Supply Chain
- → Dealing with Difficult People
- → Effective Meetings
- → Communication Skills
- → Facilitation Skills
- → Managing Upwards
- → Giving and Receiving Feedback
- → Consumer Behaviour
- → Delegation and Empowerment
- → Basic Economics for Managers
- → Finance for non Financial Executives
- → Business Forecasting
- → The Marketing of Services

Management Briefs
Essential Insights for Busy Managers

Our list of books already published includes:

→ Be Interview-Wise: *How to Prepare for and Manage <u>Your</u> Interviews*
  Brian McIvor

→ HR for Line Managers: *Best Practice*
  Frank Scott-Lennon & Conor Hannaway

→ Bullying & Harassment: *Values and Best Practice Responses*
  Frank Scott-Lennon & Margaret Considine

→ Career Detection: *Finding and Managing Your Career*
  Brian McIvor

→ Impactful Presentations: *Best Practice Skills*
  Yvonne Farrell

→ Project Management: *A Practical Guide*
  Dermot Duff & John Quilliam

→ Marketing Skills: *A Practical Guide*
  Garry Hynes & Ronan Morris

→ Performance Management: *Developing People and Performance*
  Frank Scott-Lennon & Fergus Barry

→ Proven Selling Skills: *For Winners*
  Ronan McNamara

→ Redundancy: *A Development Opportunity for You!*
  Frank Scott-Lennon, Fergus Barry & Brian McIvor

→ Safety Matters!: *A Guide to Health & Safety at Work*
  Adrian Flynn & John Shaw of Phoenix Safety

→ Time Matters: *Making the Most of Your Day*
  Julia Rowan

→ Emotional Intelligence (EQ): *A Leadership Imperative!*
  Daire Coffey & Deirdre Murray